# Unacceptable

# Unacceptable

Amelia Richardson

Unacceptable by Amelia Richardson

ISBN 978-1-955136-24-2 (Paperback)
ISBN 978-1-955136-25-9 (Hardback)
ISBN 978-1-955136-26-6 (eBook)

This book is written to provide information and motivation to readers. Its purpose is not to render any type of psychological, legal, or professional advice of any kind. The content is the sole opinion and expression of the author, and not necessarily that of the publisher.

Copyright © 2021 by Amelia Richardson

All rights reserved. No part of this book may be reproduced, transmitted, or distributed in any form by any means, including, but not limited to, recording, photocopying, or taking screenshots of parts of the book, without prior written permission from the author or the publisher. Brief quotations for noncommercial purposes, such as book reviews, permitted by Fair Use of the U.S. Copyright Law, are allowed without written permissions, as long as such quotations do not cause damage to the book's commercial value. For permissions, write to the publisher, whose address is stated below.

Printed in the United States of America.

New Leaf Media, LLC
175 S. 3rd Street, Suite 200
Columbus, OH 43215
www.thenewleafmedia.com

# Contents

Chapter One ................................................................................. 1
Chapter Two ................................................................................. 5
Chapter Three ............................................................................. 12
Chapter Four ............................................................................... 17
Chapter Five ................................................................................ 22
Chapter Six .................................................................................. 27
Chapter Seven ............................................................................. 33
Chapter Eight .............................................................................. 46
Chapter Nine ............................................................................... 55
Chapter Ten ................................................................................. 63
Chapter Eleven ............................................................................ 72
Chapter Twelve ........................................................................... 81
Chapter Thirteen ......................................................................... 86
Chapter Fourteen ........................................................................ 91
Chapter Fifteen ........................................................................... 96
Chapter Sixteen ......................................................................... 102
Chapter Seventeen .................................................................... 107
Chapter Eighteen ...................................................................... 112
Chapter Nineteen ...................................................................... 123
Chapter Twenty ........................................................................ 126
Chapter Twenty-One ................................................................ 137
Chapter Twenty-Two ................................................................ 144
Chapter Twenty-Three ............................................................. 147
Chapter Twenty-Four ............................................................... 153
Chapter Twenty-Five ................................................................ 156
Chapter Twenty-Six .................................................................. 164

# FORWARD

*"Life can only be understand backwards;
but it must be lived forwards."*
Soren Kierkegaard

Life inevitably has its ups and downs, and mine has been quite normal in that respect, but nothing lasts forever, the tough times as well as the highlights are transient and holding onto this reality has helped me through a lot of the ups and downs in the fluidity of life.

Having a tough and unsettled childhood often leaves its mark and can make the rest of life a little more challenging, but I firmly believe that as long as there is life there is the potential to heal and it's never too late.

What I have written about took place many years ago, and I have spent years trying to understand the many different aspects of those experiences.

On the one hand I needed to put those experiences in the past and live in the present, and to enjoy each moment of a better life, whilst on the other hand I deeply felt the importance that I didn't want to invalidate the past by not learning from it.

Perhaps the most difficult thing for me to learn, has been to accept that one doesn't have to understand why things happen in life, or why people behave as they do, and that it's alright not to understand. For many years I thought I would be able to accept only when I understood, but time has taught me otherwise.

Of course I've made decisions in life which have been influenced by my early year's experience and not all of them have been the best decision under the circumstances, but perfection is something which is unattainable in this life and therefore accepting 'mistakes' has to become part of our empathy towards ourselves and others.

What I hope to achieve in writing this account of my life is to encourage some reflection in those who hold their beliefs very firmly, to encourage a balance of love, kindness and appreciation of fellow human-beings, who may or may not hold the same views, be those relatives of any kind, children, parents, siblings, aunts, uncles, or anyone who could be called 'thy neighbour'.

Whatever one might believe, remember to be kind to all.

# Chapter One

He was like a stranger to me and how does a six year old address a stranger who is also her father?

This was the dilemma facing me as a child of six years old.

I knew who my father was, but I didn't really know him.

I only had an impression of him from the short times I had stayed with him and during those times I found he wasn't someone who engaged with his children any more than he had to. I got the distinct impression, that he preferred to be aloof and distant, and was content to leave me to the care and attention of my older sisters.

My parents separated when I was very young, and after their separation my sisters and I stayed with either of them for a few weeks at a time. I was the youngest of the children and stayed with our mother more often than my older siblings did.

Our father would decide which of us would stay with him and which of us would stay with our mother, he would also decide how long each of those visits would be. He would often swap two of the children that had stayed with him, with the two that had been staying with our mother or he would take all of us to stay with him, and then return two of us back to our mother.

This swapping was a regular occurrence, and it was this unsettled arrangement which meant that I wasn't able to spend enough time with my father to get to know him at all.

While staying with our mother on one occasion, my sister and I were attending a small country primary school, which was small enough to have only two classrooms and two teachers, the infant class and teacher and the junior class and teaching headmistress. It was situated in a small village on the south coast of the country, in the beautiful coastal county of Cornwall, a large county lined with a ragged coast-line of rocks and cliffs.

One day our father came to the school to pick us up. The weather was warm, dry and sunny and my sister and I had enjoyed the long walk to school that morning, totally unaware that our father was on his way to see us.

The door to my classroom opened during morning lessons and the headmistress called me out.

"Your father is here to see you" she said with a mixture of authority and concern.

I knew this meant that the headmistress had given her permission for me to leave school for the day, and that I wouldn't return to finish the school day, which I would far rather have done, and that I would probably be taken by our father to his house, not knowing when I would return to our mother and to this school.

Following the headmistress down the corridor, I saw my father approaching.

I was going toward him from one direction, from the infant's classroom, and my older sister was approaching him from the other direction, from the junior classroom.

I didn't know how to greet him, what to say to him, or even what to call him, and noticed that my sister was approaching him with excitement and a confidence I wish I had.

There was a warmth in her approach, as she called out "Oh, Daddy!" above my more timid "Paul!"

His whole demeanour toward me instantly changed, instead of greeting me as he was about to, he deliberately turned away from me and hugged my sister.

I immediately realised that I had said the wrong thing and was so disappointed in myself, and very disappointed not to be greeted by his hug.

I knew instantly I had used the wrong name and that I had addressed him incorrectly and that he really wanted to be called "Daddy".

But I had used logic!

Ill informed infant logic, but logic nevertheless.

Our mother had very recently, told us to stop calling her "mummy" and to use her proper name. If we ever did say "mummy" to her out of habit, she would always respond by saying "I've got a name". We had always called our father "daddy" and I thought that since our mother had left, he too might prefer us to use his proper christian name as they were no longer "mummy and daddy" to us. But my assumption was wrong, and I deeply regretted not being able to go back in time and relive that moment of greeting my father without hurting or distressing him.

After picking us up from our school, we spent the day on the cliff-top messing around on the moorland grass watching the seagulls overhead making a noise, enjoying the bright blue sky and the peace of our surroundings, while our father continued to pursue his own past-time of reading.

He didn't speak to me that day at all, from the time he picked us up, till we were dropped off at our mother's house at the end of the day, and I was left disturbed that my father had been hurt by something which I had done to him, but also wishing that it had not resulted in such a feeling of rejection, when I was only doing what I thought would please him. I was only a child and doing what I thought was right.

If he had only communicated with me, he would have made life so much easier, but he didn't seem to want to make life easier for anyone, himself included. He always held everything very close to himself, never letting anyone know what he was really thinking.

Our mother didn't have any say in the arrangements regarding which of her children stayed with her, when we came and went, or how long any of us stayed with her. It was our father who had the transport and the means of travelling back and forth, and it was our father who decided where we would be and when.

Neither of our parents had phones to communicate with each other, or for us to communicate with our siblings when we were separated, or to keep contact with the parent we were away from.

My father was outwardly a very quiet man, but carried a presence with him which was quite striking. Somehow, without saying a word he was able to change the atmosphere wherever he was.

But as a young child I found him rather awesome, cold and unapproachable and someone I sensed one shouldn't either argue with or question, and certainly someone not to contradict.

There was an aloofness about him, almost an air of the untouchable.

# Chapter Two

After a long and tiring train journey north, my sisters and I arrived in Scotland in the Spring of 1970 to join our father and two brothers who had gone on ahead.

This move meant that we were now a very long distance away from our mother who had remained in the south of the country, and although we would now be living permanently together, we would be living permanently without her.

I was 7 years old at the time and the youngest in a family of six children.

Up until now there had been so many moves in our lives, many different homes to settle into and many different schools to attend, that we had learned the only way for us to cope with all these changes, was to live one change at a time.

But this move was different than the previous ones. This move brought us all together, all the siblings moving together into one place and not split between two parents.

Our first night in Scotland was spent in a bed and breakfast where we found things very different.

We were introduced to biscuits which were coarse, hard and thin but which were called cakes. The cakes we knew were soft and sweet, it was biscuits that were hard and thin. These were definitely hard biscuits, but called oatcakes. Cakes!

"What dictionary was used up here in Scotland?" we wondered.

And their cheese was orange! We had never seen orange cheese before.

We were greeted in the morning with "How's yourshelves?" which we thought was very funny because it's not hard to say "selves" and the really proper way to speak was to say, "How are you?"

Shelves were something on the wall that you put things on!

"They definitely used a different dictionary up here."

Adding to our surprises, after supper the lady of the house called us all into the sitting room where we followed her example and sat quietly, wondering what was about to happen. She then put a small hat on! Her husband came in, taking a book in his hand which he read from, they then proceeded to get up, turn around and kneel down with their heads in the chairs they had just sat in!

Timidly we followed and copied them.

Then we heard a soft voice rumble, as the father began a long quiet talk to someone who wasn't in the room!

This was indeed very different to anything that we had experienced in our lives so far. The practices were different, but most of all the atmosphere was different.

Intangibly different.

The house we moved into a few days after arriving in Scotland was a modern bungalow overlooking the playing fields of the local primary school. It wasn't a large home and the seven of us just about fitted in the space.

I entered our new home one day when everyone else had gone outside, and a fear of the empty open space completely gripped me. I was paralysed with fear, heat rising in my stomach and twisting like a hot tornado.

Maybe it was the many changes and experiences in my early life that left me vulnerable to fear. All I knew was that if something was in front of me, I was willing to face whatever challenge it brought but anything which I thought might be behind me, put me into a state of petrified fear.

Here, all alone I was facing nothing and no-one.

I was frightened of the nothingness and all the imagined possibilities that the openness provided.

But there was nothing in front of me now, and there was no-one else in the house, there was just me, and it was that, that really frightened me, being all alone and vulnerable. Most of all I was frightened at what might be behind me, so I put my back firmly to the wall to make sure nothing or no-one could surprise me from behind and without taking my back from any surface, I passed cupboards, doors and walls, and eventually made my way through the house, passing our father's room without moving my back from any surface, but I was not being able to find what I was looking for.

I had an instinct that something was "up" and I wanted to find out, but I was unable to free myself from the supporting walls in order to look around properly.

A sadness came over me as I glanced out and saw my sisters playing happily with some girls in the school playing fields, the school we were sure we would begin attending at the start of the next term and pre-empted friendship with some of the children.

I were very disappointed when the start of the new school term was imminent and our father told us that we wouldn't be going to this school, and in fact we wouldn't be going to any school at all.

We had to accept with disappointment and dismay what our father wanted.

I had so loved going to school, and loved learning and I preferred being in school than in the many homes I had ever been in.

I loved school meals, the sound of the little milk bottles making their rattle in the crate as the milkman delivered them fresh every day, I loved the tuck shop with biscuits or sweets.

I loved the smell of crayons and pencils, I loved doing arithmetic and learning spelling.

School provided a routine in an otherwise chaotic life.

Now I would have none of this to enjoy? What were we going to do?

He told us that the Bible said that we (females), should stay at home, and that by keeping us at home, he was doing what God had directed.

The boys, however would be allowed to continue going to school, which was now secondary school for them as they were teenagers.

We didn't live very long in that house which we were glad about, as we girls really didn't like watching other children in the school playing field, doing what children do, playing around with their friends and having a normal life, knowing it was something we were never going to enjoy again.

After a few months in our first home, we moved again, but this time into a beautiful property not far away, which we shared with a friend of the family, who came to live with us in the capacity of a tutor/housekeeper, and who had bought this new home for herself and for us to live in.

We settled easily into this most idyllic house standing in an acre of ground with extended gardens, trees, lawns and a small orchard.

The house was approached by a long gravel lane which branched out from a very quiet country minor road. Set in the middle of fields and on the border of a forest, it was very quiet and peaceful. In the distance was the view of a Scottish mountain over which the sun glowed, forming exquisite shades and hues of light.

The property consisted of an old farm cottage of two-up-two-down, but had an addition of a two-storey extension of a kitchen and bedroom on one end. There was a large whitewashed barn which was divided into many different areas, a basement, an open-ended byre, three hay lofts, a workshop area, and a milking parlour. In the acre of ground there was a large kitchen garden to the rear of the house, and in the front there was a small lawn edged with beautiful perennial borders and space for fruit trees beyond the lawn. The whole of the property's border was lined with many different types of trees; conifers, silver birch, copper beech and beech, fir trees and spruce.

The barn provided space and shelter or us to explore and play in, and in the summer the wooden lofts provided a warm and comfortable space to spend time.

However, for me it was a place I only went into when I felt courageous as I still held memories of being alone in our previous home and the fear that I had experienced then remained very real. I much preferred being outside where there was plenty of space around me, and didn't like being hemmed in by walls and ceilings.

I spent many happy hours roaming the garden, the orchard, the lawns and surrounding fields and being free to roam in youthful, happy abandonment.

We sometimes wondered about our mother, and how she was getting on. She sent us cards and presents in the post, things which she made, or things which she thought we would like. My favourite was some Japanese tissue paper flowers, which opened up when put into water. I was fascinated by the delicacy and beauty of the fine paper folded and into tiny shapes, then opening out into exquisite flowers, as if by magic changing their appearance in absolute silence.

Our father's bedroom/study was downstairs in the house, in what would have been the parlour and consisted of his fast-growing collection of books, his bed, desk and a couple of chairs. It was somewhere we never went unless invited by him, which usually meant he had something very serious to say.

One day he did call us all into his room and the four of us stood quietly in front of him, each with our own thoughts as to why we were there, and wondering what change we might need to brace ourselves for again.

He started talking and interrupting our thoughts.

He told us that from that day on, we had to treat our mother as though she was dead.

Dead!

A small explanation was given to us.

She had been immoral, had broken the marriage vows, and therefore in God's eyes she needed to repent and we needed to disregard her, so that her soul could be saved by her repentance.

We were stunned, but dared not question his thoughts or decision.

Back in our own bedroom, we reminisced about our mother, and together we each shared our different experiences and memories we had of her.

She most certainly wasn't dead to me, she was alive in my heart and to be expected to treat her as though she were dead was painful.

How could we be asked to live a lie, to think a lie?

According to our father "God" had said so, and we had to believe that that was reason enough.

From now on, the Bible would be the rule book, and we had been instructed to be obedient, as that was our God-given duty.

The only thing that mattered now, as far as we knew, was that the "right" thing was being done on principle, according to the Bible and the Bible was the word of God the creator, and therefore the lawgiver, to whom all must obey or fear retribution.

I struggled between wanting to do what I was told was the right thing, but also not hurting my own mother and treating her unfairly.

Wanting to please the parent I lived with and who used God in their reasoning, won over in the end.

We were soon put to the test, and would our affection for our mother guide our actions, or would we be able to implement what we had been told to do and "treat her as dead"?

One sunny day whilst playing in the garden and oblivious to any trouble brewing, we heard a car coming along the stony driveway. An agile woman got out of the passengers' side. I sensed a bit of confusion among my older sisters who seemed to see something I didn't.

They saw our mother jump out of the vehicle!

Our mother!

We were supposed to treat her as dead and now she was right in front of us very much alive and lively!

The oldest sister went immediately to our father for instructions as to what to do and soon returned with them.

We could talk to our mother, we could wander around the garden with her, but she was NOT to be allowed into the house.

Being still a young child I was attached to my mother. I had spent most of my life with her. I remembered vividly being looked after by her. She had been a prominent figure in our formative years, and now? She was here, but not quite here. She was part of me and I was part of the family, but she wasn't part of the family. In a very deep place I had conflict, sadness, bereavement and a feeling of falsehood – not living the truth. Conflict, unspoken, unshared, kept hidden in the depth of my young heart and emotions. I was confused by my love and emotions toward my mother, and those towards my father and the principles he had committed us to.

But I needed to focus on the moment, on today and do all I could to share as many aspects of my new life as I possibly could with my mother during her short visit.

We took it in turns to talk to her and show her around the garden and the outbuildings, we sat outside together on the garden bench and chatted about anything and everything. She left, not having entered the house, but having had spent time with each of us individually and gained an idea of how settled we were in our new home.

I was approaching my 8th birthday. I didn't want to turn 8.

I wanted to stay 7. My father had said that 7 was God's special number and I wanted to remain in God's special number.

However, the day inevitably arrived and 8 I became with no more connection to anything special.

# Chapter Three

For the first time in our live's, family life had become relatively stable.

We had settled in well with our tutor who had come to live with us and whom we grew to love, learn from and rely on.

She had known our family for a long time and now took on the role of caring for us as we grew up without our mother.

After so much disruption in our early years, our father and tutor aere happy to give us a respite from stress and allow us to be free, to be children. I spent many hours playing in the garden, sitting under the trees, roaming the fields and watching butterflies fluttering around, birds flying overhead, and young shoots coming through the ground underfoot.

I simply loved this freedom, freedom just to be a child and let go of all the built up stress, worry and uncertainties which had dominated the past eight years.

I learned to ride my brother's old bicycle which was far too big for me, and to make imaginary farm yards and fields in the dusty gravel using his matchbox farm vehicles. When he came home from school I would be delighted to show him what I had created that day, and we often added imaginary fields and lanes, creating them as lines in the dust and pushing the toy tractors along them, bringing in the imaginary harvest or ploughing the fields.

In spite of the wonderful freedom I was enjoying, I missed being at school, I missed the friends and the challenges that attending school brought.

I missed seeing the teachers' red marks on my work book, the "well done" comment and large tick at the end of a page, the corrected arithmetic and the hurdle of doing the wrong ones all over again.

I was growing up fast and although I loved the freedom I was enjoying, I also wanted more structure and learning in my life than I was getting, so I decided to give myself a focus – a reason for going out into the wild grass of the fields and the long grass of the lawns.

Desperate to learn, I decided to set my own challenges. I got out an atlas and set out to learn the rivers and mountain ranges of Great Britain. The longest and shortest rivers in the world, the hottest and coldest places of the earth including the wildlife inhabiting them, and I learned to identify everything I saw around me– caterpillars, butterflies, grasses, flowers, birds and trees.

But the one subject I couldn't do by myself was maths. I just didn't know how to progress with learning by myself and I soon tired of the endless repetition of doing what I already knew.

I soon reached an impasse and any initial enthusiasm of setting myself learning challenges soon wore off.

Disappointed but realising my own limitations, my invented 'school lessons' were discontinued, and I had to find other ways to occupy and challenge myself.

Our breakfast was the same every day, and consisted of enjoying as many slices of freshly baked brown wholemeal bread as we wanted to eat, spread with a thick layer of black treacle. Lunch would be the same as breakfast, bread with either treacle or sometimes cheddar cheese. We loved it.

After occupying ourselves for most of the day, we were expected to be ready for dinner at 6.00pm where we would eat the main meal of the day in relative silence, gathered together around the dining table. The food was good wholesome cooking, done by our tutor and which we all enjoyed.

Our table manners had to be impeccable and correct at all times, there could be no slouching, no elbows on the table, no noisy eating or scraping of the crockery, no slurping, and holding all cutlery properly, definitely no talking at the table and no eating before the head of the table starts. The dinning chairs were wooden carved oak seats with tall backs and no arm rests, and we had to maintain a straight and upright posture at all times.

We would often play out to the garden after supper, enjoying the evening sun with the idea we might sleep better if we 'ran off' our meal.

But one day after we had finished supper, our father told us to stay at the table, while he went to his room and came back with a large grey tome in his hand, and finding his bookmark he started to read to us.

After a while, I fidgeted a bit on my chair, which was at the opposite end of the dinning table to where he sat.

The wooden chairs we sat on, had a habit of creaking and squeaking and as I fidgeted my chair made a quiet but rather obvious creak.

After a few of these creaks happened, a look of disapproval in the form of a heavy frown came directly at me from my father, giving a silent but overt message of disapproval.

I had to guess what had caused my father's look of displeasure.

As long as I kept the creaking of my chair to the bare minimum, I avoided my father's intimidating looks of displeasure.

The next day he did the same, he read after supper and again the next evening, and so he formed a new routine, and we didn't go out to play after supper ever again.

He often read for hours without stopping, and as a child of eight I was expected to sit still for whatever duration of time he decided he would read to, and that was often till midnight and beyond.

Most of what he read I couldn't really understand or appreciate and certainly couldn't relate to at all, it was completely above my understanding and interest.

The first book he read to us was a commentary on a book in the Old Testament, The book of the Prophet Daniel, which describes dreams and visions which Daniel had, as well as being the Prophet made famous by being in the lions' den.

He read about the dreams of statues which the Prophet Daniel had, and about what those dreams and visions could possibly mean, not about the exciting story of how Daniel escaped from the lions' den, and I was very glad when the commentary on the Book of Daniel was completed.

Over time the readings changed from Biblical Commentaries, to sermons and expositions of theology, such as the difference between the parents having children baptised and an adult being baptised, and the difference between Roman Catholicism and Protestantism, the different types of church governments and the theology and arguments for each set up.

We had the whole of the Doctrine of John Calvin explained in minute detail. The 'Regulative Principle' was thrashed out and adopted, we heard much about the place which woman should have in the family, in the church and in society.

I certainly learned how to sit still and listen to things I didn't understand and to stretch my physical ability almost to beyond, to stay up late and be tired, and not to speak my thoughts or feelings.

I had learned to accept and adapt to whatever I had to, in order to get through what was expected of me.

The Bible, the Authorised King James version, was held up to us as the book for rules, values, practices and principles.

It was the guidance our father endeavoured to use in all his actions and he taught us that the Bible had everything we needed to know, that it contained a true account of the beginning of time and the beginning of the earth, that it included maths, if one cared to notice the significance of numbers and the way God used numbers in his order of things, that it gave a perfect set of rules for the order of society, gave instruction on how to bring up children and it even included prophecy of how the world will come to an end.

Anything one really needed to know was there – everything else was regarded by our father as 'unnecessary' for his daughters to know.

The passage which was used to guide his decision about our education was Titus chapter 2 verses 4-5 "teach the young woman to be sober, to love their husbands, to love their children, to be discreet, chaste, keepers at home, good, obedient to their own husbands".

We were to be taught to fulfil the directives in these verses and everything else which he decided about us and our education was with these directives in mind.

So not surprisingly, among other things we were tasked with doing all our own washing which was done by hand, as there was no washing machine in the house. Each one of us was given the responsibility to wash their own clothes, including our own bedsheets.

When I was first given the task of washing, I was eight years old and was too short to stand at the sink and pull out heavy woollens and bed sheets, so I was exempt from those items, but I did have to wash everything else I used.

I tried to economise on my washing load and keep my clothes as clean as I possibly could, but found it hard when I loved being outside in the mud and dust so much.

In keeping with the Biblical guidance of our education I was also taught how to make the family's Sunday dinner, which was not a 'Sunday roast' but was a large Cottage pie, large enough to feed the eight of us.

I learned how to finely chop the onions, brown off the mince meat and season, peel (very thinly) and mash potatoes. I was not expected to put the dish in and out of the hot oven, that was something our tutor did, but I was taught how to tell when it was ready to serve.

I enjoyed this task and spending rare time on my own with our tutor, I felt as though I was being useful and appreciated, and nearly every Sunday I made the dinner until our routine and family life was rudely interrupted again.

# Chapter Four

Attending church became very much part of our life and constituted most of our social interaction, and with church attendance came Sunday school.

I was young enough to go to Sunday School and was happy to be with other children my own age again, and especially to have a teacher, someone I could call "*my* Sunday School teacher"

This would mean having lessons again!

Accountability!

Class-mates!

Above all, learning.

Our local church was fairly small, but well attended, the whole congregation almost filling the church at the beginning of the Sunday morning service.

During the singing of the third Psalm, which was just before the 40-45 minute sermon started, the children and teachers would leave the service in the main church and go into the vestry for their lesson. They would then all return to the main church just before the last psalm was sung by the congregation.

The Sunday school was generally only attended by children of primary school age and I was young enough to be in the infant class!

To young children all adults generally seem old, and to me my teacher seemed very old, but she also very pleasant and approachable. She would read each week from a book of bible stories and then hear us recite a catechism question and answer. She then concluded the class with a prayer, and we would file back into the main church service and rejoin our families.

The catechism we learned was the Westminster Shorter Catechism (1647) of 107 questions and answers which is set in the language and style of that era.

By the time someone was old enough to leave the Sunday School, they were expected to have learned at least the whole of the shorter catechism, and maybe start on the larger catechism.

There is something about reciting to a teacher in front of others which somehow cements things in ones' memory and I found it a very effective way of learning.

The custom in the church was for all females to wear a head-covering when they worshipped, according to St Paul's letter to the Corinthians were he states that a woman should "pray having her head covered".

Now we realised, why the lady in the bed and breakfast on our first night in Scotland put a hat on during family prayers!

Now we also wore hats to church!

And from now on we were not allowed to have our hair cut, it being "a shame for a woman to have short hair" as St Paul also said to the church in Corinth.

The first year we attended Sunday School, our tutor, my sisters and I went to the annual Sunday School outing with great pleasure and had a thoroughly enjoyable day.

Reporting back to our father on our return we got the impression he wasn't too pleased. His disapproval was something we sensed, by his lack of enthusiasm and interest in details and his quiet grunt when told we had gone to the swimming baths. His demeanour told us what we didn't want to know and it wasn't long after that outing that he told our tutor to take our swimming costumes away from us, as they couldn't be regarded as 'modest apparel'.

The following year, we wanted to go on the Sunday School outing again, even if it meant we would remain out of the swimming baths and stay with the adults.

With the fares paid for in advance, our seats on the bus booked, and arrangements made for the bus to pick us up on the day, we waited with great anticipation and excitement for our pending day of fun and change from our daily routine.

We waited for our father to take us the one mile to the bus stop to be picked up for the trip.

We waited for him, but he showed no sign of moving himself or of driving us to any bus stop to be picked up.

Time was going by and we knew the bus would be waiting for us at the end of the road.

Then slowly it began to dawn on us, that we weren't going.

The disappointment was harsh and the painful embarrassment was acute.

Why say we could go, then not allow us?

Making us a 'no show' case of rudeness.

He gave no explanation to us about why he didn't let us to go that day and we dared not ask for one.

It was just another instance of learning to accept the unacceptable way to behave.

The following Sunday we took the bus to church as normal and we were left to answer many questions about us not turning up at the bus-stop for the outing.

"Where were you?"

"The bus waited half an hour for you all".

"Why didn't you let us know you wouldn't be coming?"

The embarrassment went deeper for us, as the lack of understanding by those who had waited for us became very clear.

What could we say?

The only explanation we could give was "Daddy said so", but that didn't really answer their questions, even if was the only thing we could say.

Our father had a knack of avoiding answering questions, and would very often leave us to answer for things we had had no contribution in deciding.

"Daddy said so" was the reason we often had to give, though perhaps we could have asked them to direct their questions to our father for an answer, as we didn't have a satisfactory one. But to have replied in that manner and directed them to our father would have been totally unacceptable and unthinkable to us.

Shortly after this event our father added to our disappointment and decided that we would no longer be attending Sunday School at all, but this time he did explain his reasoning to us, which was that children were part of a family and should not be separated out in worship, that they should be present the same as the rest of the family and shouldn't be treated differently. Children should learn from adults, and not be separated from them. God made us a family and we should be treated as one.

Every Sunday morning the children went out to their Sunday School classes while we sat through the long sermon and prayers as though we were adults. It wasn't easy watching them go out and knowing what was being done for them in the vestry.

To my young ears, it seemed as though the preacher droned on and on, using long words I didn't yet understand.

Our father never sat in the same pew with us in Church, but always sat a few rows behind, so he could 'keep and eye on us' and he would tell us afterwards if we had fidgeted too much, or whether we had looked around at other people too much or made too much noise turning pages, but he never mentioned my habit of falling quietly asleep leaning on our tutor's shoulder. When I did own up to sleeping he said that it didn't matter and he didn't mind.

Sometimes I just couldn't fathom him out - I was not allowed to fall asleep when he was reading to us at midnight, but I could sleep through a public church service at mid-day!

Then quite out of the blue as far as my sisters and I were concerned, we no longer went to this parish church, which we had been attending for about two years, and we started going to another congregation further away, though we remained in the same denomination of churches.

The reason we left, we were told years later, was that our father had wanted to become a member of the congregation and had made an application to the elders for membership. The elders wanted to ascertain what his relationship with our mother was and also with our tutor. They were not familiar with divorce then, and they wanted our father to live clearly as either a divorcee or as a married man. In fact our father was divorced and lived as a divorcee, but unless one knew us and the family arrangements, it might have appeared to outsiders that he was living with another woman (our tutor) in a relationship but not married. This was not acceptable to the elders and they were not happy with his situation arguing that he could 'bring the faith into disrepute' by his way of living and he was therefore refused membership, so he decided to seek membership in other congregation.

There was absolutely no doubt at all, in the sincerity of those who worshipped in the church in every congregation we attended.

The church was their life, and they endeavoured with all they had, to live a life worthy of being called by the name of Christ.

They were passionate, committed, and devoted to the life and customs they knew and loved.

Even as a young child, I noticed how much soul and heart was expressed not only in the worship, but also in the hospitality given to each other.

As in all families, sisters don't always get on and they sometimes argue. We were no different and my sister and I argued one day and I ended up scratching her forehead, making a visible graze mark.

Our father saw the mark and asked her how it got there and was told that I had made it. Without asking further details he made both of us write one hundred times, a verse from the Book of James 3:18 "The fruit of righteousness is sown in peace of them that make peace".

We were careful to keep all outward disagreements peaceful from then on!

# Chapter Five

We saw very little of our teenage brothers as they were either in school, out working with local farmers or doing up old cars and machines they bought and hid in the nearby woods.

Very rarely were they present at supper or any other time.

They did come to church occasionally, but as it was impossible for the eight of us to fit into the one small car we had, more often than not they were exempt from attending.

But one evening our brothers did join us for supper and we were happily squashed around the table, enjoying good food and being together.

The younger brother had been coming home later than his curfew.

Our father reminded him what that curfew was, and asked him what he thought should happen if he didn't adhere to it.

In a small voice he muttered

"Be punished, I suppose".

We were all told to take note of what had just been said between the two of them.

About a week later we were very surprised when we were all called to follow our father into the barn.

Going into the barn wasn't something I liked doing at all, though sometimes curiosity got the better of me, and I would go in and wonder around upstairs in the loft but it always felt eerie and desolate, but now I was going in with the whole family, even with my brothers!

The air in the barn was dusty, musty and damp.

The woodwork was full of holes with woodworm.

There was only fading natural light and it was cold and unpleasant.

There was a tense sense of foreboding among us as we watched our father.

Why had we been called to go into the barn with everyone? What was about to happen?

We could only wait.

If we asked our father our questions would be ignored, or maybe given the "wait and see" response, and so we had learned over time to "wait and see", and our father's demeanour on this evening left us in no doubt that any questions would remain as questions.

In the first room of the barn our father stopped us all and as we stood around, he reminded us of the words we had heard between him and our brother at supper the previous week.

Our brother had not kept his curfew and so was about to be punished.

How, we had no idea.

Why, we now knew.

We stood listening to our father giving his mandate, the "god-given directive of Proverbs 23:13-14,

"Withhold not correction from the child: for if thou beatest him with the rod, he shall not die. Thou shalt beat him with the rod, and shalt deliver his soul from hell."

Oh no, I wanted to cry.

My brother was about to be punished and I knew by the situation unfolding that it was going to be serious.

I wondered what he might be thinking, knowing what is about to happen to him.

I tried to imagine what he was going through.

He appeared to have steeled himself, more than I was able to harden myself in readiness.

We were directed to go down to the cellar.

The cellar was the worst place on the whole of the property.

It was even more dark, damp and dusty than anywhere.

The earthen floor looked as though it hadn't been swept for decades.

Cobwebs hung everywhere, thick heavy ones all over the walls, the frames, and the small ventilation holes in the walls.

The air was heavy with lack of airflow.

In the middle of this creepy, unwelcoming, unvisited, darkened, damp place was a tall meat cage made out of metal mesh, adding to the sense of doom and gloom.

We stood as close to the doorway as possible as none of us really wanted to there.

With a cane in his hand, our father announced he would be giving one strike for every year of our brother's life.

> Strike one,
> That was OK for him.
> Strike two,
> He could do this.
> Strike three,
> That hurt.
> Strike four,
> That hurt a bit more.
> Strike five,
> Wincing with pain.
> Strike six,
> Resolute not to give in.
> Strike seven
> That really hurt.
> Strike eight,
> Deep resolution.
> Strike nine,
> That was bad.
> Strike ten,
> Ow, that hurt.
> Strike eleven,
> No more, please.
> Strike twelve,
> Tears.
> Strike thirteen,
> Bent over with pain.
> Strike fourteen,
> Can't take any more, tears, bent over, crying.
> Our brother sounded beaten down and broken.

I joined the others in slowly making our way out of the dingy cellar, silent and emotional, upset and shaken at what I had just witnessed.

My heart, my emotion, my eyes and understanding were too young for this.

What I had just witnessed was too much and I held onto the hope that our brother would learn from this brutality not to get into any more trouble, and not put himself or us through anything like this ever again.

Our young hearts responded to our need for stability by being loyal to our father and taking on his belief system as much as we were able to understand it. For me at the tender age of eight, it was sufficient that God was the one respected, obeyed and pleased, that "God" said and "God" required.

Pleasing "God" was what was important.

I had learned Catechism question one:
"What is the chief end of man?
Man's chief end is to glorify God, and to obey him forever."
and that answer summed up the whole of my education.

In our new church, there was a young people's meeting which was held during the week, and which my sisters were old enough to go to, which was allowed as it was not during a family service. They really enjoyed those meetings, and shared with us younger ones what they had learned, told us about friends they had made, and the songs they sang.

We were also pleased to go regularly to the midweek prayer meeting, even though our attendance to a late midweek meeting was questioned by some members of the church, as it was most unusual for children as young as I was to go. I, on the other hand didn't have to get up in to morning and go to school! The Prayer meetings were very well attended and many of the men members would take part by praying in the meeting and the sermon tended to be a little shorter than on the week-end. We were happy in this church, having learned to sit through long services and listen to sermons with long words which we were just beginning to understand.

The minister was newly inducted to this congregation and was very enthusiastic and dramatic in his preaching, which we much appreciated as it made the long sermons more interesting, and my tutor and I were less likely to fall asleep.

# Chapter Six

Holding a wooden darning mushroom, I pushed and pulled the needle in and out, learning to darn with accomplished precision and graduated to darning my fathers' woollen socks with excellence. I was proud of my ability and training, especially when I was awarded the job of darning his socks.

His standards were exacting and being given his approval was very important to me and also meant I had attained a satisfactorily high standard which had to be maintained.

Our father always wore socks which were made from Welsh wool and spun specifically for hard wearing socks. Eventually I was taught how to knit them and I knitted all his socks for a few years, reinforcing the heels with cotton thread added to the woollen yarn making it much easier to darn as they wore out. I was taught how to re-knit the heels as well, as the leg part lasted much longer than the foot, or sometimes I would reknit the complete foot onto a leg. He liked them to be shaped very precisely and after a few attempts I managed to knit them to his satisfaction.

Our education was largely done by our tutor who was given instructions by our father as to what and how to teach us. Although she had a teaching qualification she was not employed by our father as a paid tutor, she lived with us as part of our family, having being entrusted with our care and with implementing our education. She was a very gentle lady, well educated herself and of similar age to our grandparents.

We were instructed in basic mathematics and in reading. Reading was done out loud with our tutor listening, and reading with good diction and voice was one of the most important aspects of our private education.

Slowly but surely the emphasis on our education started to change.

Everything started to become very serious and childhood games and past-times were not encouraged.

The only music we now had was the acapella singing of metrical psalms.

Reading was restricted to factual or religious accounts, but literary works such as "The Pilgrims' Progress" and "The Holy War" works by John Bunyan we were actively encouraged to read.

The novel 'Robinson Crusoe' was only permitted because of it's standard of written English, though I never had any interest in reading it myself. For me it remained on the list of 'permitted' books.

I disliked reading very much because I found it hard work, especially trying to get to grips with unfamiliar words as I didn't have the patience to build them up from syllables, and there were too many anomalies in the English language to teach oneself to read well, and I always ended up frustrated.

My reading at this time consisted of a set of children's books about famous christian people, like Florence Nightingale (the pioneering nurse during the Crimean war) and David Livingstone (missionary and explorer in South Africa).

There were plenty of books for my older sisters to choose from if they wanted to, as our father's collection was rapidly growing and we were allowed access to a section of his collection. He took an interest in obtaining first edition copies of some very old and rare books, and these he highly prized.

We also continued voluntarily to learn the Shorter Catechism, one question and answer each week and would recite these to our tutor. If we all recited our pieces correctly and fluently we would be rewarded with a large bar of Cadbury's milk chocolate to share between us.

There was an air of 'what is spiritual is best' that developed and although we were not actually disallowed, it was not considered 'spiritually profitable' to play, even in the garden. We could 'relax' with a book, but to play was frowned on.

Now, previously enjoyed games were discouraged and eventually not allowed and laughter was regarded as frivolous. After several years of concentrating on what was 'spiritual' we were allowed to have a chess board, and our father tried to teach us chess, but by that time we had lost all interest in games and it never became something we spent our time on. He had decided that it would be good for us to learn strategy and to learn to think ahead and he thought that chess was a good way to learn those skills.

But for now my times of fun had to change and become times of intensity, measured by accountability of being spiritual.

Going to church services or having visitors from the church, became the only social interaction I experienced and enjoyed, and we attended church very often, some weeks almost every day, often travelling miles to hear a preacher regarded as being conservative and a good theologian.

One evening after another long service, we had been invited back to have tea with one of the church members.

We always loved being invited back for tea.

Going into someone else's home.

Having cake!

Having a cup and saucer!

Helping in someone else's kitchen.

One such evening – a strong urge came bubbling up from inside of me.

I had sat quietly for long enough!

One service too many.

One washing-up and helping, too many.

There was a spark of life which needed to come out!

I had had enough of unrelenting theology.

Enough of endless discussions on fine points of doctrine.

I was a child and needed to be a child.

To be treated as a child.

Mischief got the better of me!

On returning to the room where the tea was being served, and where there was an ongoing discussion about some aspect of theology, I pressed the light switch, turned it off and plunged everyone in darkness!

Hoping no one noticed it was me who used the light switch, I sat back innocently on the seat I had left to do the washing up. I hoped that the weather would be blamed as electric power cuts were not uncommon in those parts of northern Scotland.

Alas for me! I was known to be the culprit immediately!

I did so enjoy bringing everyone back to reality, even for such a short time.

Expecting to be reproved afterwards by my father, I was very surprised that nothing was ever said about what I did, which left me wondering what else I could get away with!

But guessing what would be allowed and tolerated, was not worth the risk of getting it wrong, so I decided 'once was enough'.

Quiet, immaculate in person, articulate in speech and impeccable in manners, shy in public with an intellect that gained him high respect among his peers, is how I describe my father at this time. I was proud of him and of his commitment to do what he believed to be right. He had the strength to be different from the status quo. To stand up against the flow, with his own well thought-out reasons.

To me, he was rather unapproachable, but I believed that that was because I was young, and he always regarded the 'young' to be the domain of 'mothers'.

He always spoke of 'woman and children' as a unit.

I noticed my father in the garden one day, which was really unusual, unless he was mowing the lawn, and I was curious about what he was doing, so I quietly crouched low on one side of the hedge, knowing he was on the other side.

Both of us were very quiet and I wasn't sure if he knew I was there or not.

Then.

Over my head came my sister's much loved kitten!

The kitten landed on all fours with a loud screeching meow.

How could he?

How could he throw a small kitten so high? And why?

What could a small kitten do to him?

He just threw it over the hedge and didn't look to see if it landed alright!

I was shocked and left with a sick feeling in my stomach.

I felt for the kitten, and hoped it wasn't hurt.

We knew our father couldn't tolerate animals, especially cats, and my sister had been very careful to keep her kitten away from him, but why be so cruel to a harmless, little and delicate creature.

It was something I just couldn't understand and most certainly didn't like.

Part of him remained a mystery. On the one hand he had an air of respectability, but I had just witnessed a very cold and cruel act he had done, and one which I didn't think a respectable person would do.

Happy and free outdoors, but quiet and restrained indoors was the pattern for us.

When indoors, if our father could hear our voices from his bedroom/study we were called to his room and the one making the noise, had a wooden clothes' peg with a spring in it put on their tongue, as they stood still in front of him. I remember thinking it couldn't be too bad, until one day it happened to me! It was painful when left on. It was designed to be painful – to deter us from making a noise – to learn a lesson – to learn the sequence of - action to consequence, at least that's how I understood it, and it worked because we learnt to be very quiet.

We were to be of "Modest apparel" according to St Paul in the Book of Titus, and according to Moses in the Pentateuch "woman must not wear that which pertains to a man, neither shall a man put on a woman's garment".

For us this meant that we were not permitted to wear trousers, have low neck-lines, our skirts had to be no higher that just above the knee, short sleeves were not encouraged, but not directly disapproved of.

Bright colours were also not considered to be in the category of "sober".

This dress code made us stand out even among the church members who were more in-line with the fashion of the 1970's. Our head-covering was changed from hats to head-scarves which made even more of a statement.

Whichever church we attended or visited, we would file in in a very precise order, would find a pew about halfway down the aisle and sit as still as possible, wearing our headscarves and very distinct clothes.

There would be no missing the fact that we were in attendance – we simply couldn't be mistaken for any other family!

# Chapter Seven

Having our first day of prayer and fasting was something I found quite difficult.

Our father had told us one evening that we should gather together for family worship in the morning, which meant a time of Bible reading and prayer.

Immediately after having finished family worship in the morning, he gave directions about how we should spend the rest of the day. We could read but we weren't to do any activities that weren't devotional, as the day was intended for reflection, meditation and prayer.

Difficult for an active child of eight years old to do.

To be told that most of the day had to be spent reading and in prayerful contemplation was something I really disliked the sound of but I was curious to find out how I would manage it. I was a slow reader and didn't enjoy reading at all, and for me to give over a whole day to quietness and reading was likely to be anything but pleasurable, but then the day wasn't supposed to be pleasurable, in fact it was meant to be quite the opposite. It was meant to wean one from the pleasures of life, and focus on more lasting and meaningful things.

We could have as many warm drinks as we needed throughout the day, but having food would be kept until supper in the evening, when we would gather together for a bowl of soup, followed by family worship, and so conclude the day devoted to God and to self-improvement.

After a couple of hours of trying to be honest in my occupation, I was sitting in the garden patiently waiting for time to pass, and wondering how my sisters were spending the day, and wondering if they were wondering how I was spending it. I found it hard to find 'acceptable' things to do and I realised that all I had to do was wait it out, wait for the day to end and for tomorrow to come and bring back normality and life.

Days 'set aside' for the purpose of prayer and fasting were something which became fairly frequent days in our house and I became used to the challenge of exercising patience and quietness.

Some days of prayer and fasting were for specific reasons and one such reason on one occasion was the approaching deal of the Government, when Great Britain was about to join the European Union (1972) and our father believed that this was not a god-honouring agreement, so decided to make it a matter of urgent prayer, believing in the words set out in the Gospel of Matthew 17:20-21 "If you have faith as a grain of mustard seed, ye shall unto this mountain, Remove hence to yonder place; and it shall remove; and nothing shall be impossible to you. Howbeit this kind goeth not out but by prayer and fasting."

Making a family day of prayer and fasting was his response to any serious matter which concerned him.

The eve of my tenth birthday arrived and I was excited and looking forward to having friends over and getting a birthday present from them.

It was good to have something to look forward to, as this which happened less and less.

During the day my father took my oldest sister to his room for a talk, and she left it a few moments later with a look of acute embarrassment.

She had been told that she was going to be taken to our friends' house and tell them that the birthday visit was cancelled. She really didn't want to do it at all.

Why had he said they could come and then cancel?

We didn't know.

Later that evening as we were gathered at the dinner table we were told that the following day (my birthday) we would devote to a day of "prayer and fasting".

"Prayer and fasting would would replace my birthday?"

Yes, it did.

In the morning we had were told that our bowl of soup would be served at six o'clock sharp, and that we should be ready to go out immediately after supper.

We got in the car on time, dressed as smartly as we could and our father drove the familiar road to the local town.

Not arriving at the church or any house we recognised, but at an unknown location in the town, we wondered what the mystery was all about. We had no idea where we were, or why we were here or what was going to happen. For us it was a matter of 'wait and see'.

We followed our father into a glass fronted modern building. We were used to going into old stone built churches, but this building was horribly new, and had what we thought was very unpleasant architecture.

What was this place, so unwelcoming, empty and characterless?

It was nearly 7.00pm and dusk outside, adding to the air of mystery.

Walking through some empty corridors and still following our father, we eventually found a room with a few people in it.

"Many Happy Returns of the Day!" was addressed to me as we entered, hardly having enough time to get ourselves into the room.

Who were these people and however did they know it was my birthday?

I didn't want to be greeted by people I didn't know.

I felt they had invaded my privacy and my personal space.

If they knew it was my birthday today, what else did they know about us?

I certainly didn't like the "many happy returns of the day" and recoiled at the words I disliked so much.

I wondered "What's wrong with a simple 'Happy Birthday' and not try and be all fancy and flowery?" Something stuck in my throat about the whole thing and "got my hackles up" as one might say.

Nothing pleased us at all in what we saw and heard.

The ceilings were too low, the chairs were plastic and unpleasant to us, who were only used to wooden pews in church, wooden chairs at home and wooden seats and desks in school.

Tentatively we accepted the invitation to sit down opposite the strangers.

I closed up and became defensive.

I took an instant dislike to this group of people who exuded an air of self-pleased over-confidence.

I looked to my father for his reaction – but there was nothing.

It was clear to us that they were making an effort to communicate with us, and equally clear to them that we were not co-operating at all.

The first thing we were told by one of the strangers sitting on the opposite side of the long table which was set between us and them, was that we probably wouldn't understand a thing of what was going to be said, but we were required to be there anyway.

Ok, I thought, that was the queue for me to shut right off and pretend I wasn't in this cold, strange place and for a reason I had no idea about.

The panel of strangers talked on and on and eventually they turned to the oldest sister and asked her a few questions.

I was getting very tired.

I just wanted the day to end.

It hadn't been the best day.

Finally, the strangers turned to us and thanked us for attending.

The meeting was over.

Back home we mulled over our impressions of the meeting in our shared bedroom. We all felt the same. None of us liked any of the strangers, especially the woman in the middle of the row who did most of the talking, and we hated to admit she had been right, we hadn't really understood it.

We had to accept what we didn't understand and hoped for the best that what had happened wasn't going to be harmful to us.

Our father explained later.

It was about us not going to school.

So these strangers were trying to decide about our education!

These strangers were part of a Children's Hearing Panel who wanted to ascertain whether we were being educated.

We were not attending school and they wanted to make sure we were being educated satisfactorily, even though earlier in the year our father had been called to court to answer for his actions regarding our education, and he had won his case to teach us at home.

The judge who had ruled that we could be kept at home had retired, and the Local Education Authority had reapplied to a new judge who had referred the case to the Children's Hearing.

It was not illegal not to go to school, but it is illegal not to educate children.

Our father strongly believed in Civil Rights and wanted to exercise his right as a parent to bring us up in the way he considered to be right.

He believed that we were being educated, and were being taught the things we needed to know.

He didn't want us to learn things which he believed were not only unnecessary, but things which were not according to his understanding of what God required.

He also strongly objected to being told what to do with his family by a woman, and especially by a woman, who he was sure had no belief in God.

He was keen to inform us that the law as set out in the Education Act 1944 stated "children should be educated in state school or otherwise" and he was doing the 'otherwise'.

Though I was glad to be assured we were not breaking the law, the finer point of the difference of 'education and staying at home' was lost on me.

All I wanted was for us to be left alone for once, undisturbed and grow up just a little bit more.

A week later we each received a letter!

This never happened!

We each opened our own to find them all the same, just addressed to each of us personally.

We had received summons to attend another Children's Hearing in a week.

The summons ended with the sentence "if you can't read this, give it to your parents"

Really! If you can't read it, you can't follow the instructions! Who really needs to go to school?

The irony wasn't lost on us.
Nor the irony of being summoned at all?
How were we supposed to get there?
Drive ourselves?
Arrange our own transport?
Ask our father to take us?

We were somewhat amused but also a little bewildered at what to us seemed a preposterous situation. We were minors and the Children's Hearing Panel should surely be dealing directly with our father and not with us.

The letters we received were handed to our father, who took them in silence.

The summons were legal summons which carried an arrestable offence if not complied with.

They were 'illegal' as far our father believed and he had no intention whatsoever of us attending.

And neither did we.

To avoid the possibility of us being detained for not attending the Children's Hearing our father decided to take us away, out of the area of the jurisdiction of that particular Education Authority, the day before the Hearing was due to take place.

The four of us packed ourselves and a few items into the car and our father drove to – no-where. Just away.

After hours of driving the long road south, we stopped at a service station for food, a leg stretch and some rest, With some food in front of us and sitting round a small table in the cafe area, our father bowed his head and offered thanksgiving as was his custom in a low soft tone.

Someone came over to us.

A stranger.

We were cautious of strangers.

So far strangers in our lives hadn't been a good thing, remembering as we did the effect it had on us years before, being taken from our beds in the middle of the night by strangers at a very early age, and more recently strangers trying to disturb us enough to satisfy themselves about our family life.

So who was this stranger?

We watched our father's reaction to him very closely, and all seemed congenial between them. So far, so good.

After a few words were exchanged between them and a handshake given, the stranger went back to his seat, we finished our food and then went on our way.

The next part of the journey was also very long, until we were told that we would be visiting our grandparents.

I squealed with delight – with excitement.

I was immediately told to be quiet.

I may have remained quiet, but my anticipation remained bubbling inside.

I had the idea that grandparents were loving, and people who could be trusted. They were part of our family and I was very happy to think that soon I would be with people who had a love and care for us.

We arrived at our grandparent's home and received a warm welcome with hugs, and were very glad to be out of the car after twelve hours being cooped up and quiet.

After four days of rest and food, and getting to know our grandparents, we headed out again, like fugitives on the run.

We ended our journey this time in Wales in a small holiday home overlooking the sea, and which belonged to the stranger we had met in the Service station.

The stranger who had taken an interest in us, and who, after hearing of our circumstances had offered us the use of his holiday house.

Perhaps some strangers could be angels as well.

Our father told us that we were not to be seen there, through windows or doors, we were not to go out or talk to anyone, so that our whereabouts could not be reported back to the Authorities.

Being in a holiday house, there wasn't much food left in the cupboards and we became hungry after a day with almost nothing to eat, grateful though we were for the haven of safe accommodation.

You can't keep young healthy children inside too long, and one day before our father got up in the morning and against his instructions we went out.

We walked the coastal path and with a degree of shyness we bowed our heads each time we passed another walker, hoping not to be recognised.

The sea air was so good! And the exercise was so good!

After that escapade we felt able to be kept quiet for another stint, the next stint which would take us back home on another 12hour drive.

A week after the Hearing was due to be held, and having stayed in the holiday house for a few days, our father thought it was probably safe to go back home, and of course we couldn't stay away indefinitely, wondering around the country with no possessions or place of abode.

On the way back home we saw blue lights flashing in the distance which alerted us.

Blue lights meant emergency services, and the police were forefront in our minds as they were the ones who had the power to detain us, and we really wanted to avoid being detained at all costs.

There was probably a road accident ahead, but we had to drive on, and as we drove past we saw that the lights ahead were indeed police lights and we were very afraid of being recognised.

Only about 30 miles to our home, and our journey would be over. We felt so near, yet so far.

So much could happen in the next few miles.

We had travelled all the way from Wales without being noticed.

In fact we had travelled all the way from North Scotland to South East England then to Wales and almost back again without incidence.

As we passed the flashing lights our father told us to "Put your heads down, as low as you can" to reduce the risk of our faces being seen and recognised. One man driving solely in a car was less likely to be identified, as the family of four girls who hadn't answered their court summons.

No doubt the police force had been put on the alert to look out for the girls who had absconded from court summons the previous week.

Even if we weren't recognised we knew the car might be, but there was nothing we do about that.

It was too late to take another route home.

We passed the flashes, the officers, the ambulance and the cars without being stopped and were very relieved to be on our way.

Leaving the scene behind us we arrived home in the early hours, a little exhausted and worried but so grateful to be home again, to be in our own beds, in our own space and with our own personal things at hand around us.

We were so happy to be back with our tutor again, and to know from her that no-one from any legal authority had come looking for us while we were away.

We were glad and relieved that she too was safe and well.

A sense of security set in as the next day emerged and unfolded.

We had come through the trials of the past week, and now wanted everything to go back to normal.

Then – in the afternoon we heard a car!

Immediately retreating to our bedroom and keeping quiet, we waited to see who had driven into the yard.

We were still on nervous alert not knowing how long the authorities would search for us or how long we were 'arrestable' for not answering our summons.

Sneaking a peek out of the bedroom curtains, two policemen were seen knocking on the door.

Our sense of alert increased, and our reaction was to be even quieter.

We recognised one of the policemen as being one of the officers who were at the road accident only twelve hours earlier.

They were invited in and to our surprise our oldest sister was called down to make tea for these policemen!

What was going on? One day we do all we can to avoid them, the next day they are having tea in our home?

The rest of us were called out of our room a little later, and we now stood in front of our father, our tutor and the two visiting officers.

Our father said

"They have come to 'arrest you', and take you to the police station".

The arresting sergeant and his deputy led us out of our home and into the yard, where we piled into the police vehicle and were escorted to the local police station, passing as we did so, the church we had grown to love so well.

The irony!

The irony was, that the sergeant who now had us in his charge attended this church just like we did.

Arriving at the police station we were all put into a small room which was very stark and bare. Apart from our chairs and a table there was nothing.

No windows, no pictures, nothing but bare walls and a closed door.

Time dragged, as we tried to occupy ourselves. We had nothing to do but talk to each other. We shared our worries, our concerns. We sat in silence, each steeped in their thoughts. Day dreams were created and changed, friends invented and lost.

All the time we knew that we were each trying to hide the real fear of the unknown.

Four very long hours later, we were interrupted when the door was opened by someone - someone wearing a pink shirt!

Well, for us that was the limit!

A man in pink!

Pink was for females.

Pink was the colour even we weren't allowed to wear.

A pink shirt and a pink tie!

We took an instant dislike to this person, especially when he tried to be so very nice to us.

On the one hand being 'nice' which we found offensively and artificially 'sweet' and patronising, while on the other hand putting us into this situation, we found it inconsistent and hypocritical in our state of raw emotion and uncertainty. We would far rather he told us up front what was happening without trying so hard to gain our confidence, which we were adamantly determined he would never manage to get.

We knew each other very well, as we had been put together very closely for many days and hours. We shared our thoughts and feelings with each other, so our reactions were of a kind.

This man in pink introduced himself by giving us his name and then told us that we should go with him – "don't be afraid, I work with the police and we've decided where to take you – come along".

He knew we were very reluctant.

We were reluctant.

Did our father know what was happening to us? No one told us where he was in this event.

We thought of him as our protector, our point of reference.

What would he expect of us? Would we do the right thing without him there to tell us what to do?

At least we were in this together and we drew comfort, resolve and strength from each other.

A journey of twenty minutes in this stranger's car found us in the car park of a building with a sign which read 'children's home'.

Not for the first time in our short lives had we been inside a 'children's home' and some of those memories were happy ones.

Meeting us in the quiet hallway was the matron, but there was no evidence of any children anywhere.

We didn't feel safe not knowing what was happening to us, or how long we were going to be here in what was called a children's home but which had no children in it.

Much to our delight our father arrived shortly after we did.

We were very glad to see him and he even brought items from home for us, things which we would need for an overnight stay and having this contact with him and having some of our personal things with us, helped to relieve our sense of insecurity.

We sat together in one of the family rooms, had supper and then engaged in the family worship which had now become an invincible part of our family routine. We discovered then that there were children in the home and they were sneaking a look at our worship and asked us many questions afterwards.

Our father told us to be compliant with the authorities, and to do what we were asked by them with respect. We were glad to be instructed by him on how we should respond to what was happening, and to have his reassurance that we had responded an appropriate way.

So finally the authorities had got hold of us and were going to get what they wanted. They were going to find out for themselves whether we were being educated at home or just staying at home.

They wanted to be absolutely certain that the law was being adhered to in their jurisdiction and there was only one way to find out.

After a peaceful night's rest we were taken by 'the man in pink' as he became known to us, back to the town where our meeting with the authorities first took place just a month before, to that distasteful looking building with its distasteful memories.

However, today we were being separated from each other. I was taken into a small room, not dissimilar from the police cell where we had spent the previous afternoon.

Our father had briefly mentioned to us once that the authorities might want to put us through a test to assess the level of our education, and I now realised that I was now going to being tested by them to find out if I was being educated satisfactorily. I really didn't want to let my father down and fail to answer correctly any questions I should know, but I was nervous and my thoughts were with my sisters as I knew each of them were in the same situation as I was in, and I knew that we were in each others thoughts and I gained strength and resolve from that knowledge.

I was ushered into a very small room by a woman who didn't introduce herself and who I had never met. She invited me to sit down, in a tone more suitable to a command, as though I was obliged to accept her invitation.

I sat on one side of a desk with the stranger on the other side, in this tiny room with just the two of us and her about to embark of some sort of interrogation of me, a small and vulnerable ten-year-old.

I found this stranger to be cold in her manner, and she told me nothing about why we were there or what she was about to do. There seemed nothing to her, so I couldn't like or dislike her, but I did resent very deeply being separated from the rest of my family and being asked things which seemed to me to be quite irrelevant to the moment. But I was determined to rise to the occasion and do the very best I could.

I had no idea how the test was being structured, I was just being asked one question after another, and also had to do some reading out loud which I dreaded. I soon noticed that the questions got harder and harder, and then I understood how the test was being structured. It went from simple to hard questions, and wherever I started having difficulty in answering correctly that was the level I had reached in my education.

Although determined to do my best, I knew at the end of the test that I had let myself down a bit. I had been too nervous and unsettled to do my best.

My mind wasn't on the questions which I was being asked, and which I knew the woman sitting in front of me knew the answers to, but for some reason wanted me to tell her anyway. My mind and emotions were with my sisters and worrying about them and asking in a very deep place, why all this was happening and what was really going on, and where was our father, and these seemed far more relevant questions to me and to my survival than the ones I had answered just moments before.

Relief flooded into us, as we were reunited with each other in the foyer and were told we were free to go back home!

Words from heaven itself.

We went home and mulled over what we had each been through, and we all felt as though the test was taken in conditions which were unfair to us, and that none of us had performed as well as we could have.

We would now have to wait and see what their verdict would be.

We were all tired and on edge, not knowing what the next upheaval would be or when it would happen.

# Chapter Eight

Less than a month later another summons arrived for each one of us, to attend another Children's Hearing.

So once again we were on the road!

This time we were more prepared, though not any the less stressed and our Grandparents were again our destination.

With them we felt safe, and a long way away from the disturbances taking place at home, and being with them gave us was a sense of stability and peace.

We had arrived to another warm welcome at our grandparent's and spent a restful night with them.

The day after our arrival, our father went away all day, and he arrived back just as Grandma was setting the supper table.

We sat down around the dining table with a wonderful spread of food, when Grandpa came into the kitchen, and pointed with his thumb to their front room and said directly to our father in his uniquely gruffly low voice

"Visitors for you"

Grandpa didn't look at all pleased.

Slowly we continued to eat as much as our nerves permitted, wondering how there could be "visitors for you" when nobody knew where we were, not even our tutor back home.

Grandma then told us that she had received an anonymous phone call earlier that day, asking if we had arrived safely, the caller refusing to give their identity when she had asked for it.

We asked Grandma to describe the voice of the caller, and we immediately guessed who it might have been – it sounded like 'the man in the pink shirt' by her description and just the sort of 'sneaky' thing he would do.

How we disliked him so.

Rightly or wrongly we decided it was he who had betrayed us.

Having gone into the front room to see the 'visitors' our father came back into the kitchen visibly disturbed and angry, with a palpable and stoic level of self-control.

Addressing us he said "finish what you are eating, and don't take any more. The police have come to arrest you".

We could barely look at each other, let alone look at our grandparents.

We knew just how annoyed, disturbed and angry our father was, because for once he didn't rush us to get ready.

We went upstairs to collect the small amount of things we had brought with us and he decided that before going downstairs to the impending arrest, we would sing a few psalms and pray together to calm us all.

We took our time.

In fact we took lots of unnecessary time.

But the inevitable had to happen.

Downstairs we went to face the officers and our fate that lay in their hands.

Following behind our father, one by one in the orderly manner we were used to we went into the hall.

"Mother" he called, much louder than normal, and loud enough for the officers in the front room to hear.

"Come and say goodbye to your granddaughters, as they are being arrested".

"Whatever for?" she said.

"For righteousness' sake" our father stated.

Turning to the waiting officers, who were by now facing the open door ready for action our father said,

"Come and arrest them then"

"No surely, we won't do that" came the immediate response.

"Well if they are not arresting children from their grandparents home, what were they doing" was the look we gave each other.

We wondered if 'arresting' had a different meaning in England than it did in Scotland.

Or was this answer given out of the discomfort of the officers taking us away from this very peaceful village, where everyone knew everyone else, and most people had been resident for decades, like our grandparents had?

Whatever the reason, the answer stood as we had heard it, and was a response which made quite an impression on our young minds.

This time, our mode of transport to the police station was a police van. We were 'put' in the back and driven to the local town, our father following us in his own car.

Again we sat for hours in a police station waiting for someone, somewhere to make a decision about us, but this time our father was waiting with us and although his presence would normally add strain to the atmosphere, we were very glad to have him with us right now.

With a decision made and accommodation found for us, we were driven by the police some distance away and arrived at a large, old, imposing and very unfriendly looking building, which was an institution for children. It was used for housing either delinquent children who had a criminal past, or children who were just waiting for the 'system' to organise their future.

We arrived on Thursday evening, and were told by the staff, that as Friday was a school day we would be expected to attend 'school' on the premises.

Hearing from the children that 'school' was in a small wooden port-a-cabin in the garden and that apart from the three r's, the children were left to fill in their own time, we were satisfied that we were not going back on everything our father stood for, or what we were going through because of those principles and beliefs which he held.

The resident children asked many questions, the most important as far as they were concerned was, "Why are you here", "What have you done?" and we soon learned that this, to them really meant, "What crime have you committed?"

On hearing the reason why we were there, the children couldn't believe, like we couldn't, why it was us, and not the adult responsible for us, who was being detained.

Most of the resident children staying here were very tough and appeared not to be all that well looked after, with old clothes, mangled hair and a rough manner. A lot of them couldn't read properly and seemed to have no self-respect or aspirations. They were however very capable of fighting for themselves and knew how to survive in the system.

It was a rough and sad place.

The policy of the Institution was for a GP to check over all new arrivals, and we were declared by the examining medic as "the healthiest children he had ever seen".

We were chuffed with that!

In the morning we were told that we had visitors in the reception room and there, to our absolute delight was our father and grandmother. It was great to see them and to hear our father giving us reassurance that he would do all he could to get us back.

This visit made a huge difference to us, lifting our spirit and resolve.

By Friday evening we were beginning to get worried about how our situation was going to be resolved as we had heard nothing since our arrival or our father's visit about what was planned for us by the Education Authority.

We wanted to be home, and not in this place which had a dark and dismal air about it. It felt a place full of conflict and anger. The children were angry being there, and the staff were angry with the children, and this vicious circle of resentment pervaded everywhere.

No, we needed to be home.

But nothing was happening as far as we knew, and a fear of being left here too long was starting to become very real to us.

We hung onto our faith and prayers that all would be alright in the end. We reminded ourselves of our father's commitment to his principles and held onto that example, but the 'authorities' did need to make a decision quickly about what to do with us, as this was a place the resident children frequently ran away from, and which idea was growing on us, especially feeling as we did, that we had no good reason be here at all.

Late on Friday evening, almost after we had given up hope of hearing anything that day, we were told to be ready to leave at 6.00am the following morning.

We were leaving, and going in the right direction – away from here – and going home!

We were woken by the matron very early on Saturday morning, while it was still dark and the other children were fast asleep, and after a very brief breakfast we went outside and were met by officers who took us to the local railway station. At the station we were met by another set of strangers – strangers who would accompany us all the way back to Scotland.

These strangers were three woman who gave us the impression that they really didn't want to be doing their job, and who didn't want to be with us at all and certainly not travelling all day – in a train.

But then neither did we want to be with them!

They said very little to us. They didn't introduce themselves to us and made no pleasantries to make us feel more at ease, so they remained strangers in every way, and strangers who we grew to dislike more and more as the day went on.

We were once again with people who knew who we were, but we didn't know who they were.

Resentment built up and we were very unhappy with our unsympathetic escort.

Getting fidgety after several hours on the train, our only activity was walking the corridors or going to the toilet, but even doing this we were told that if we wanted to use the toilet we had to been accompanied by one of these strangers.

As though we would attempt to escape out of a moving train!

We longed for someone to be sympathetic to us, to see things from our perspective, to understand what we were going through.

After all, we were still only children.

We weren't criminals and had no intention of being criminals.

All we were doing was being obedient to our father.

We were obedient children.

More obedient in fact than our escorts!

Such satisfaction we had!

One of the woman, I can't call them ladies, lit a cigarette in the carriage, and one of us shyly pointed out that there was a 'no smoking' sign in the window.

"Oh, don't take any notice of that" she said.

So why did she hide her cigarette every time the guard passed, if what she was doing was perfectly in order?

We were surprised at this blatant disregard for obvious regulations. Such behaviour would never have occurred to us!

Whoever these people were, we were perplexed to discover that they were less law-abiding than we were!

After many hours of being cramped together, we approached the end of our journey with these strangers. It had become a very stressful situation for all of us, and being confined together in an atmosphere which was palpably awkward took it's toll. In all honesty, we would have preferred to have spent those twelve hours cooped up in the car with our father.

We had nothing to do all day but look out the window, watching the passing countryside and the endless stations coming and going, and reading our ever constant companion, the Bible.

As darkness came over the countryside, we could no longer be entertained with the passing views and we knew that just a little more patience and we would be home again, so we eked out the small amount of what we had left and stretched it to the very end.

Finally the train stopped to our enormous relief, as we thought that our tortuous journey with these strangers would be over.

However, after alighting off the train, we were very carefully manoeuvred into a waiting police van. Joining us in the back was the woman who had smoked against the regulations (yes, we were keeping tabs!) and the other two women sat in the front with the driver who was very obviously a policeman. We were not told where we were being taken or why it needed four officers to take us.

On the way to our next destination, which we were sure would be home, there was an incidence which meant the driver of our vehicle got out and used the police radio and he ask the woman who sat in the back of the vehicle with us to help him, by communicating on the radio – identity now revealed! She must be a policewoman to be able to use the police radio. A plain-clothes police woman!

Really?

Why not tell us? Why the secrecy? Did we not deserve the truth?

And why had she been so ready to disregard regulatory notices herself?

"God help the rest of us, if police officers set that kind of example!"

'Hypocrite' was the only word we could use to describe this act of selfishness and we were left with a very distasteful sense of injustice.

Finishing our journey with no further incidences or revelations, we were very disappointed to find ourselves parked outside a youth hostel – and not our home.

We were outside one of the youth hostels in the same familiar town which our church was in. Disappointed not being taken home, we nevertheless were glad that we were not far from home and that we were also in a town where we knew people and were not strangers.

We had learned to find the bright side of whatever situation we were in – it was the only way we had come through so much.

However, we knew nothing about what was happening to us now and why we were taken here and not taken to own our home just a few miles away. To us it seemed as though we were pawns in other peoples' hands to be put here, there or anywhere as they pleased, and not treated like children who would appreciate a certain amount of understanding about our own movements.

One of the most difficult things for us at this time was not knowing where our father was, and not knowing if he knew of our whereabouts.

We were settled into the youth hostel that evening, and the next day we were delighted to receive a telegram from him, which meant that he knew where we were.

The telegram simply read: "Joshua 1:9".

We looked up the reference in the Bible and it read:

"Have not I commanded thee? Be strong and of a good courage; be not afraid, neither be thou dismayed: for the Lord thy God is with thee withersoever thou goest."

We took heart from knowing that he had sent us a message.

Even though not in his own words, the point was not lost on us that he was presenting the bible in every aspect of his life and directing us to so as well.

As soon as he was able, our father visited us in the hostel together with our tutor. We were delighted to see them and they brought us some much needed clean clothes from home. He couldn't give us information about what was happening, other than there would be another children's hearing scheduled soon and we were waiting for that to be arranged.

Although we were not allowed to go out or off the Hostel premises, we were allowed visitors and were delighted when the minister came to see us – our minister, as we could now call him, having joined the congregation a few weeks earlier.

Becoming a member of the church required giving a testimony of one's living faith in Jesus, trusting in his sacrifice on the Cross for the forgiveness of one's own personal sins, committing to and agreeing to live a life honouring to the Lord, and this testimony was given in front of the elders of the church, followed by being given the 'right hand of fellowship' if they agreed.

We had presented ourselves for membership and been received just a month before this visit from the minister.

So much had happened in the last month.

It was less than a week since we were taken from our grandparent's home and only six weeks since our attendance at that first and memorable children's hearing on my tenth birthday.

We were now awaiting for another hearing to be called, and we had to stay in the hostel until we had attended, whenever date that hearing would be called.

It was set for the following week and we left the hostel with all our belongings together to attend the hearing, hoping more than anything that we would be able to go straight back home afterwards.

After the hearing we sat outside the room it was held in, waiting and waiting to be told something – hoping for something good.

And we got it!

We could go home!

Whatever happened in that room while we waited, didn't matter immediately to us, we were so delighted to be together again, at home with our father and tutor.

The most important thing was that we were together and we were to be hassle free for three whole months!

The result of the test, to decide our level of education, was that our education was found to be adequate in most areas, and on the grounds of that result the Children's Hearing Panel had agreed that we could stay at home on condition that we would be put through a particular curriculum and would be tested again in three months, to which our father gave lip service.

We weren't put through any other curriculum than the one we'd had all along!

Our father's decision was intractable.

He had his principles, and no one would interfere with them, with him or with his family.

# Chapter Nine

In the Bible it says, that the 'day of one's death is better than the day of one's birth' and taking that on board, our father decided there would be no more birthday celebrations in the family and this included celebrating the birth of Jesus at Christmas, so Christmas came and went as any other day of the week.

Along with many other christians he took literally the account in Genesis of how God created the world in six days and made man (Adam) in his own image and made a woman out of the man, so women were understood to be the 'weaker vessel' and were to be in submission to the man, and in acknowledgement of that submission women were to have their head covered in worship.

Our father took the 'submission' part much further than most christians, and he applied it very vigorously to every part of our lives.

Whatever our father decided to do and everything he taught us he could rationalise, explain and justify from his understanding of the Bible, which added to his air of authority. He taught us that he was only implementing what God had directed.

A peaceful three months passed, and almost to the day, we received a summons to attend another Hearing.

This time, to avoid our whereabouts being found out, our father knew he had to go further than his parent's home in England. So we set off, each of us with a few personal things, and squashed into our small car, we crossed the ferry to Ireland.

We spent days driving aimlessly around both Northern and Southern Ireland, with nowhere particular to go and no-one to visit.

We meandered around the towns, villages, lanes and roads, visiting a few church buildings to help pass the time, and surviving on bread and cheese.

We felt safest in Southern Ireland, knowing that we were out of the jurisdiction of British Law there, and that we were not in the 'system' as absconders.

It was a war-torn country in 1973, full of checkpoints and soldiers who often stopped us, searched the car, and asked what we were doing in Ireland.

Avoiding being taken into custody!

We could hardly say that could we!

Soldiers were everywhere – even at the entrance to residential streets. They carried large rifles, and tension was very tangible.

Everywhere there was unrest and distrust.

We learned to by-pass the soldiers, worrying that someone might know about us, recognise us and report our whereabouts.

Had that not happened unexpectedly before, when we came across the accident returning home?

We trusted no-one.

After a few days of travelling round Ireland, we headed back home.

With relief at arriving back home and the noise of the tyres on the roads still ringing in our ears, and after being cramped up in a small car for almost a week, we listened to our father's instructions for the time ahead.

On no account must we let anyone know we were home.

We mustn't go near the windows, or answer the door to anyone, not even the postman, and if anyone did come in, and were let in by himself or our tutor, we were to go immediately to our bedroom, taking all our stuff with us, leaving no trace of ourselves behind, and remain quiet in our room until we were told otherwise.

This was not fun.

This was becoming very serious and affecting our childhood, our lives, our sense of security and freedom, even our normal development of needing to play outside, laugh together at a normal volume and even to talk together normally.

Life became very serious.

Our childhood had gone.

Another hearing was arranged in place of the one we had so recently missed and we received the summons to attend.

Those distinctive envelopes delivered by the postman and our reaction to them started to become very familiar, mixing in us a sense of fear, frustration, annoyance and injustice.

We no longer opened them, but handed them immediately to our father and he never told us the date or time of the scheduled Hearing we had been summoned to attend. There was nothing we could do about the summons anyway, so there wasn't any need for us to know. We were completely dependant on our father and tutor and rightly so.

Our father decided to sit the next one out at home.

The day came and the weather was inclement with a heavy fall of snow, the driveway dangerously full of freshly fallen snow flakes which made it very quiet and consequently we didn't hear the vehicle drive down as we normally would have.

We heard a knock on the door.

We did as instructed, curbed our curiosity and stayed well hidden and quiet in our room.

Gathering up any evidence of us recently being in the house, was similar to what we had imagined the Jews felt, who were hidden in houses during the 2nd World War, and who we had learned about as our father read us accounts of the rise of Hitler and the persecution of the Jews and Christians. Them and us treated as criminals, fugitives and wanted, hiding in a home, on the run and not betraying ones' beliefs, family or heritage.

We strained to hear what was being said by the policemen at the door.

"Are the girls in?"

"I can't tell you" our tutor replied.

"Are they here?"

"I can't tell you".

"Do you know where they are?"

"I can't tell you".

Hearing the answers our tutor gave to the inquiring police officers, we were proud of her, and admired her resolution not to give them any information as to our whereabouts and so they left with nothing.

Not with us, or any knowledge of where we could possibly be! But they weren't finished with us at all.

Surmising they would return with search warrants, our father told us to eradicate any trace of us having been in the house recently.

We used the skills we had learned from our tutor, cleaning our bedroom carpet with a damp cloth, making our beds flawlessly, tidying up all our personal belongings which we each stored under our own beds. We hid any dirty washing, made sure that the bedroom sink had no toothpaste or brushes on it, no flannels hanging on the sink hinges, no rubbish in the bins and above all, opened the windows to eliminate any residual smells.

Gathering us in the hallway, we were told to put on warm clothes, wellingtons and coats and to follow our brother who was told to "take us away, anywhere – just away, away from any roads or dwellings."

There was a sense of urgency to get out. We had taken precious time in tidying up and the officers were sure to be back with their search warrants.

We were all determined to be safe and not give ourselves up.

All bundled up as best we could, we headed out not knowing where we were going, how long we would be away, or when we would get our next meal, though we felt sure we would be back before evening and certainly before darkness fell.

The snow was lying thick on the lawn as we set out from the cottage door and the warmth of our home.

Luckily there was one set of footprints in the snow, where someone had walked across the lawn earlier that day. We all tried to walk in these footprints, just in case the officers would be interested in counting how many sets of prints there were leading out of the house, thereby concluding that we were indeed somewhere in the area and had been in house that day.

We walked on and on for what seemed like ages, our brother taking the lead and the rest of us following closely behind in no particular order.

It was bitterly cold, and the snow was so deep in places, that it came over the top of our wellington boots and melted in the warmth of our feet, but then the water inside our boots felt as if it had got even colder, like it was beginning to freeze.

Slosh, slosh we went with every step.

Slosh, slosh, squelch, squelch the water went in our boots.

Our brother was very sympathetic and realised that we could no longer walk in the same footsteps as each other. He allowed us to stop and empty our boots as often as we needed, although he did maintain a sense of moving forward and going somewhere – where that somewhere was, none of us actually knew.

We were beginning to get on edge with the situation, and started to slow down, but also realised that we had to keep going forward, even if it was only very slowly, so pressed on despite the incredible discomfort.

We were walking in a newly planted forest of young trees which were planted in ridges and straight rows, but the blanket of snowfall had made the ridges disappear and become like one complete covering. The weather was overcast and the whole scene was one of a pure white blanket of snow with snow laden clouds overhead and snow covered branches weighing heavily on the young tree branches. All we could see was the same scene. Endless snow changing the landscape with its own paintbrush.

All around us was made unidentifiable by the weather conditions and we were lost, in what was normally a familiar and recognisable place to our brother.

But now, one row of young pine trees looked just that the next row, and the next row and the next.

The new plantation was flawless, the trees being the same distance from each other and the rows of trees the same, made finding landmarks or navigation extremely difficult, especially in overcast weather full of heavy snow clouds.

The snow had made a blanket cover and the ground appeared to be one even level, when in fact it was full of ridges. Walking on uneven ground when all you see is deceptive smooth evenness on the top and in front of you is very hard work and after a while, I found this aspect of the walk too much for my short legs and I started to lose energy, co-ordination and heart.

Discouraged and extremely cold my spirit was starting to wane and I felt I was too small and unprepared for this advanced adventure.

What we heard was what we needed to force us to keep going and to give up.

We heard barking.

Barking dogs in a snow-laden forest didn't make sense, so we immediately thought that the police had their dogs looking for us, this thought was enough to make us very much afraid and feel as though all our hard efforts were about to be in vain.

We could definitely be found by dogs, no matter how hard we had tried to cover our path in the snow.

No doubt about it.

Our response was to set our resolve firmly and to keep going further forward together, alongside our resolve was our sense of vulnerability, our vulnerability to the dogs, the police, the education authorities, the weather, the impending darkness, and whatever else might want to come and get us.

The barking came and went away as mysteriously as it started, and we put up a sigh of thanksgiving for our safety.

As the daylight faded along with our spirits and energy, we unexpectedly came across a recognisable feature in the forest, an old wooden tower which had fallen on its side, and we tried to make a shelter for ourselves from surrounding branches which we gathered and shook the snow from, but exposing our hands to the cold air to pull branches, became too hard so we were only able to do it for a short time, and before long we decided it was better to huddle together to retain what warmth we had.

It was now much later in the day than we expected to be out. It was fast getting completely dark and we were still a long way from home, very cold, very hungry and with no idea what to do or where to go next.

But we had to do something, we couldn't stay where we were for too much longer and be safe in the cold.

Having huddled together to retain what heat was left in us and after some discussion, we made a decision to move on hoping for the best.

One big difference between our brother and father, was that our brother's way of leading was to discuss things with us, and not just tell give us the conclusion with no opportunity to ask anything. Our decision after a very short discussion was, that we would all walk to a certain place in the forest which our brother knew, he would go on back home from there and find out what was happening while we would stay in the forest waiting for him to return with news.

We moved on with a sense of purpose – our walk was beginning to come to an end.

Surely we would be home soon, in the warmth, dry and fed.

On the way out we found a track in the forest which made walking a whole lot easier than walking on the plantation ridges, and it was a great relief for all of us as we had become almost too tired and cold to lift our legs over the ridges properly.

Our ease was short-lived as we noticed movement ahead in the dusky shadows.

We knew it!

The police were indeed in the forest!

We had heard their dogs, and now there was one walking toward us.

One lone figure walking with a torch.

We were caught and there was nothing we could do about it.

Slowly the lone figure came towards us and slowing we continued to walk forward towards the lone figure in trepidation of who we were going to meet.

I felt completely defeated.

All this effort in the freezing cold, the tiredness and the hunger amounted to nothing.

We may as well have stayed at home and been taken from there.

Lost in nervous thought and despondency, I was quickly pulled back into reality by a voice,

"That's Daddy"

There was only one person that walked like he did and our sister recognised his unique walk.

We were so happy that it was our father and not the police. We were safe, for now at least and that's all that mattered to us.

We had already learned to cope by living one moment at a time and it was very useful now to put this lesson to use.

Our father made sure that we all sheltered off the path, still nervous of who might be around, and he opened up the thermos flask he had brought with him, filled with soup our tutor had made ready for us.

This was the first time he had ever put the youngest first when he said

"Give it to the youngest first to have some".

But it was far too hot for me to drink. It was impossibly hot.

We added snow to cool it down, then more snow, tried again, then more snow.

It was still much too hot, so our brother had his share first and the others having their own share after him. In the end I was the last one to have some and by the time it was my turn I could manage the temperature and I enjoyed what was left in the flask.

After the soup was finished our father pulled out from his pocket a bar of chocolate, his favourite dark Bournville chocolate, and shared it out between us all.

# Chapter Ten

Our father soon informed us that the police had indeed been back to search the premises for us after we left, and now decided that our brother should now go back to the house and find out if the police had returned again after our father had left to come and find us. He was to ask our tutor to pack a small case with some essentials in it for us, as our father had decided that it would not be safe for us to return to our home that night. Our brother was then to meet us at a certain point in the forest with the suitcase and with any news he could get of how the police were getting on with searching for us.

So we weren't done yet! We had so hoped that we could have gone straight back home.

Although very grateful for the sustenance our father brought us and the reassurance of his presence, we were disheartened that we still had to continue walking in the dark and cold with our wet clothes on, and still not knowing when we would be safe.

After having walked in the exhausting cold for another hour or so, we finally reached our father's car which he had left parked by a gate while he had entered the forest on foot to find us.

By the time we reached the car, our brother had gone home and had returned to us in the forest, with the news that yes, the police had been back again looking for us after our father had left, and they had even stopped at neighbours asking if we had been seen by anyone.

Before getting into the car, we emptied our boots of water and were very surprised at how much water had collected. We had been walking with wellingtons full of water from the melted snow for so long that we hadn't even noticed it any more.

The suitcase our brother took from home with our essentials in was put into the boot of our car and our brother was then told to return to the house, get our shoes, and meet up with us again at an agreed rendezvous place and time.

Taking a very circuitous route avoiding all main roads, we arrived at the home of a young family who we were acquainted with, who were quiet living and newly moved to the area, so were little known by people who knew us, so

we felt moderately safe in their house with them.

This family took us in as we were, very wet, very cold and very hungry, and we were extremely grateful for their kindness in accommodating us, arriving so unexpectedly and in such dire need of immediate attention as we had done.

This was the rendezvous place for our brother to meet us and to give us our shoes, and also to give us an update on the activity of the police who, he said were still on the look-out for us.

Having confirmation that the police were still searching for us our father didn't feel safe staying in the vicinity, so after receiving warm drinks, an opportunity to dry out a bit, and a boosting atmosphere of family life, we piled once again into the car and drove off into the dark, cold night.

Mile after mile in darkness, and in clothes still damp from our recent 'walk in the woods' (as we came to call it), we huddled in the back of the car, ducking our heads under the cover or our coats whenever another car passed until, in the small hours, we parked in a lay-by and our father took some time to rest.

We were tired too and leaning on each others' shoulders we also took some much needed rest as well.

Our life, even if it was "for righteousness sake" was not very easy.

All we could do was to live each moment at a time, be survivors, be strong, resolute and above all stick together. We knew we had to give and receive strength from each other, and cause our father as little trouble and stress as possible.

Sitting quietly in the car, keeping our thoughts to ourselves was part of 'giving as little stress as we could' to our father.

Personal needs, such as food and drink and going to the toilet were not a priority during these journeys and was something over which we had learned a lot of self-control. We never asked to stop for one persons' need, but waited till all of us had the same needs.

During the past recent journeys we had learned what behaviour was expected of us during long drives. We had learned the art of quiet reflection, speaking only when necessary, our own thoughts and observations being our only entertainment.

There were no such things as puzzle books, reading books, mobile phones and apps and certainly no talking to each other unless absolutely necessary and then only a quiet whisper.

Sometimes one had to dig deep, very deep to find thoughts, but they would be there. thoughts were always there.

I managed to find some entertainment reading the name on large vehicles passing on the motorway.

My reading was poor and the one word I really struggled with was *Vehicle*, despite the hundreds of times we passed the notice *Long Vehicle* on the road I had difficulty reading and pronouncing it. It would be so much easier to have read *Long Lorry*, even though when a very young child I had a problem with the word lorry, I would say *rolly*, changing the r's and l's.

But eventually I managed to learn once and for all, the word I disliked so much, disliked for its spelling and disliked because I only came across it on long and tedious journeys. I was chuffed with my personal achievement, which I had managed with no help from anyone else!

After resting and driving for some further long hours, we arrived with the dawn, in London, outside the home of someone our father had met not too long before.

It was too early in the morning to knock on the door, so we stayed in the car outside for a 'shut-eye' and a couple of hours later we were given a very warm welcome.

Food, drinks, warmth, hot water and a bed each, even if it was on the floor!

We were taken out the next day by our host and shown some sites of London, not the normal sites which tourists see, but those connected to the history of the Evangelical Church.

We went back to a dinner of roast meat and vegetables!

The fact that they could afford to live in London and provide this sort of food was not unnoticed by me and made a deep impression. I took note and subconsciously made a comparison.

These were people who believed the same as our father, but yet they had a completely different family life – different atmosphere, attitude and relationships with each other.

Interesting!

After much needed rest and care, we piled back into the car and left the metropolis, and it's interesting life behind us.

Never being told where we were going, we whiled away hours in the car reading sign posts and guessing where we might be headed.

What better way to learn geography?

This time, the sign posts were for the West Country and then Wales.

We headed for Fishguard, to the ferry crossing to Ireland.

Our sister suffered sea-sickness badly and we knew from experience that this crossing to Ireland would not be without its challenges.

Arriving in Ireland we had no-where to go.

We just needed to be safe, and this time things were a little more familiar to us.

We travelled through the South of Ireland, sleeping in the car some nights, which could be cold and very squashed, and which I found quite frightening, feeling that the car was exposed to the elements or could be an easy target for the bombs or rifles which were known to be around in Ireland at the time. I wanted to feel safer, than what cover our car provided, I really wanted to be under some solid bricks and mortar.

Leaving the South, we headed to Northern Ireland.

The Border wasn't straight and we weaved in and out of the countries for a few miles, each time with a prayer that we would cross safely and not be unduly stopped and questioned by the British soldiers who were implementing British rule and therefore had the authority to take us away should they be ordered to so.

Being in a church community which looks after its own was useful, and we visited a few people connected with the church, in Northern Ireland whose names and addresses had been given to our father, and we found the Irish hospitality given to us from these kind people, very great helpful, comforting and necessary.

They asked a lot of questions, but then who wouldn't, given what they themselves were going through? They were as shy of us, as we were of them, but we had our faith in common which overcame some more natural reactions.

Not being confident to stay in one place for long we travelled around wondering the lanes and roads, viewing the countryside, and visiting more church buildings to break the monotony.

This journey was the hardest so far. It was aimless in destination and length.

It was still winter and very cold.

After almost a week since leaving, we started to make the long journey back home again.

More long tiring hours in the car.

Happy to arrive home with no worrying incidences during the journey, we relaxed once again in our own space.

Peace, tranquillity and calm were short-lived as more summons were delivered to us, though obediently not received by us!

This was getting beyond living without harassment.

We were beginning to feel more and more treated like criminals, (our idea of how criminals are treated).

What would these new summons mean for us?

What could we to do to make the authorities understand we were NOT going to go to school?

We were children, and just children, who were trying to grow up normally, recover from very disruptive early years and more importantly children whose main aim in life was to please and obey God.

The summons had been received and the date and time set, so once again we squeezed into the car, the car we now knew so well and headed out away from home.

We had to get along with each, being put together so often and for such long periods of time, always having to be quiet and still. This journey was no exception and it was with great relief when it ended in a small Welsh village, some twelve hours and more after we started the drive, and we arrived outside a holiday house, which was to be our home for the next couple of weeks.

Our tutor followed shortly after, by train and we welcomed her with love. Our father left us in her care while he returned to Scotland on his own.

Having our tutor with us gave us a sense of security – an adult with us and one who wasn't on any Government 'wanted' list.

She loved us and we loved her and she didn't rule us with the same austerity that our father did.

I couldn't help but be as much of a child here as I could.

I played by the stream for hours looking for smooth stones to skid across the water or just to keep for keeps' sake and climbing trees with gusto.

Lots of fresh air, just I as liked it.

Lots of freedom to do what I wanted.

I invented an imaginary friend to play with, to talk to, but talking only of what was happening in the moment, never unearthing anything which lay below the surface.

Living in the moment and dealing with the pleasures of that moment and leaving everything else was important and the way I had learned to handle life.

Our father made connection with a Baptist church a few miles away, shortly before he made his return home and going to the chapel and getting to know the congregation had a huge impact on all of us.

The services were a little different from what we were used to.

There were hymns, and an organ to accompany the singing.

We had become used to unaccompanied Psalm singing.

I so much preferred hymn singing to the psalms!

The "O for a thousand tongues to sing my great Redeemer's praise"

to

"Lord in Thy wrath rebuke me not"

The Welsh singing their much loved hymns, joining in natural harmony, with the organ vibrating the floorboards with confidence, was quite a new experience and one which I absolutely loved.

I was moved by the music and the 'hwyl'.

I was able to relate to the words of the hymns better than I could to the words of the metrical psalms although I had grown to value the Psalms very much.

The children in this church were given Bible passages to learn and repeat in the main Sunday service in front of everyone and we soon joined in the learning, but honoured our father's view of woman not 'speaking in public' and so repeated the passages we had learned, to a couple of the church elders and did so in the Sunday School rooms which were in the church basement.

The services were familiar to us in their structure of prayers, reading, sermon, prayers and singing, which went a long way to make us feel more at home.

The minister here had the same theology in the main as we were being taught, but the presentation I found much easier and more gentle.

The emphasis being slightly but profoundly different.

In Scotland and at home the emphasis, as absorbed by my young ears and heart, was much about the greatness, the majesty, the all-knowing, ever-present, holy, perfect God who was so above our wretched (a word often used in our father's prayers) sinful nature. There was a very deep sense of awe portrayed, awe at the chasm between us and God. Between sin and perfection and the theology of hell was ever present.

Here in Wales, it was more about "we love him, because he first loved us" love God because of his love to us, love being the motivation, the love of God for us as shown in his son Jesus, should melt our hearts.

The fervour and passion in preaching were familiar, and the commitment to the doctrine of Calvinism I recognised.

In Scotland we attended church and heard the preaching, but lived our own lives at home, while here in Wales, the congregation had an opportunity to show us their faith in very practical ways, as we were shown kindness in every possible way, having arrived with only enough things to last a few days, and being in a house which needed vacating after a couple of weeks.

It was not long after we arrived that we were given everything we needed.

One of the first boxes to arrive for us from members of the church was a box full of unused old computer paper.

Paper!

What a child could do with paper!

And loads of it – so much we would never run out!

Such luxury!

Someone else lent us their mini-bus for as long as we needed it and our tutor drove us to and from church in this rather old rickety bus which had its own temperamental nature.

But we loved it.

It represented love to us and trust in us.

We were given crayons, pencils, notebooks, food and clothes.

We were lent books to read, and above all and the most important for our loneliness, we were given company and friendship. In all we were provided everything we needed for the months we stayed in their care.

Most weeks we were invited to have Sunday lunch with different members of the church, either together or split into groups and we were able to make friends with children our own age.

After lunch we would join the Sunday school, which was held in the church basement. My age group did some colouring while discussing bible stories the teacher guiding our knowledge and understanding.

In all I felt relaxed and happy.

Life was more normal and that's all I wanted, to be normal.

We had been the children not going to school.

The children wearing headscarves.

The children with a private live-in tutor.

The children without a mother.

The children with a father who had no job.

The children who wore very old-fashioned clothes.

All the descriptions could be summed up as, the children who did not have a 'normal life'.

Here we were accepted and I wasn't aware of questions being asked about why we were there or how long we were going to stay.

All I remember is having a sense of being accepted, understood and cared for at the right level.

It was here that I had a new experience. I was taken into a shoe shop, and had my first pair of new shoes bought for me. I had always had hand-me-down's, so I was very shy and nervous to have my feet measured professionally in a shop and overseen by a someone else's father. I had made friends with a girl from church, and while playing together one day she asked me about my shoes which were old, scruffy and too small for me.

Unknown to me she had repeated this to her father who found it in his heart to meet my need.

Such was the kindness we experienced!

The winter in which we had arrived turned into spring then into summer and we knew that before too long we would have to be reunited with our father in Scotland and continue the life that we had there.

The four months we spent with the help of these good people seemed a long time, much longer than it actually was, as we absorbed every moment, lived every moment to the full, not looking back at what had just happened, or what might yet happen when we returned home.

We would quite happily have stayed.

But -

We had news from home that there had been no more summons since the last one in February.

It was now June and our father decided it would be safe for us to return home, and came down to fetch us.

We said a sad farewell our new friends, the place we had been the happiest for a long time, the church we had grown to love and feel at home in, the warm fellowship of those who had supported us without prejudice since our arrival and we made our way back home, each carrying and guarding their own precious memories with them.

# Chapter Eleven

Back at home we settled somewhat back into our past routine, but were disappointed with the decision our father made, which was to sell our home and he started the process shortly after we got back.

Our father wanted to get us out of the area and jurisdiction of the particular Education Authority he was more and more at odds with. I wondered if my father felt a bit defeated by the authorities, and I really didn't want him to give up now, after we had been through so much together because of his commitment and it would only be a matter of time before we would reach school leaving age – our oldest sister was almost there already, and one by one we would follow in quick succession.

It was tough letting go of the home which had provided so much for us and had brought us together in so many different ways, and I envied the family who would have this as their home after us, and after many viewings the sale was completed.

Our father didn't buy another house, in fact the only accommodation he had ready for us to go to was a small holiday house which was unoccupied for a few weeks before the holiday season started, and so all our belongings were put into storage and we were only allowed to take enough things with us to last a few weeks.

He told us that 'the Lord would provide' for our needs.

The holiday house we went to had no garden and was much smaller than we were used to. It wasn't easy living in cramped quarters with little to occupy us

as we just waited for a new and better accommodation and for our belongings to come out of storage.

I spent more time climbing trees and wondering along the stream at the bottom of the yard. I sensed an air of depression in the family, but couldn't exactly place it. There was a quietness, and rather heavy atmosphere pervading the house and I sensed a feeling that we didn't really have a sense of direction or purpose, which put us all on edge and made me want even more, to stay outside for as long as possible.

Our tutor had moved with us to this small house, still maintaining her position as teacher, mother-figure and housekeeper, but not long after we arrived she left her position with us quite suddenly.

She might have told our father what was happening in her life, and there might have been discussions between them, but nothing was relayed or said to us about her departure.

Although we had known that 'something' was brewing as she often appeared with tears in her eyes and was able to do less and less, we had no idea what was actually happening in her own life, and as children are by nature, we were so tied in our own lives, to even think she had a life of her own to live. We had known her and her husband when they were married, but didn't really know what had happened to their marriage, so we could only surmise that she was upset about something to do with her relationship with her husband.

Her sudden and unexplained departure was like a bereavement to us. She had always been in our lives and then one day she was gone, and we didn't know if we would ever see her again.

We now had to manage without her, without her mediation, advice, knowledge, organisational skills of running a household, shopping, cooking and being mindful of our needs.

I had become so used to different situations, circumstances, places and conditions that her leaving didn't disturb me as much as the fact that she left without giving us an explanation. One of the ways for me to cope with yet another loss and more change was to close my mind and emotions to it and not to think of any possible consequences it might bring to us as a family, or to my position and responsibilities in the family. I just accepted in silence, in what might have appeared as a cold, uncaring and selfish way, but it was the only way for me to continue and embrace life as it was unfolding.

After another year and a stay in two more places our father found his 'forever' home.

It was a large grey stone-built house which was owned by the church, and which had in the past been used as a manse for the local parish, but as two local parishes had been joined into one, it was no longer required as a functioning manse, and was rented or let out at the discretion of the church elders.

It was situated in a garden which was divided into several areas by stone walls, some very tall, making a complete divide and others were quite short, allowing for a good view of the garden.

In the outside walls of the house there were very obvious signs of the old 'window tax' as several of the original windows were blocked up with local stone, but still very visible – a feature which I found quite ugly.

The entrance was by a heavy door which opened into a large hall. There were several rooms that led off the main entrance hall. To the left was a room of bare floor boards, two windows which overlooked the garden, and a very small fireplace opposite the door which seemed hardly big enough to warm a cupboard, let alone a room as large as this one. The trade off in this room was having the light from the two windows, and the coldness which having two windows created.

Opposite the front door was the one and only bathroom in the house, which was just big enough to hold a bath, a sink and a toilet, with a small cupboard under the ever damp window. There was no radiator and it was always a cold damp room no matter what the season was.

Next to the bathroom was the kitchen and the door was situated at the bottom of the large winding staircase.

The kitchen here, as in most homes was the hub of family life. The entrance was to the left of the room as one entered, and on entering one was immediately facing the end of the sink unit and draining board. Opposite the door was the old cream coloured rayburn which was quite small considering the size of the house. Next to the rayburn was a cupboard where we kept cleaning things, including utensils and buckets of fuel for using on the rayburn. Our electric cooker was next to the rayburn.

All the crockery and food was kept in the one dresser which stood against the wall opposite the sink.

In the middle of the room was the large oak dinning table with the chairs which we had spent so long sitting on years before. Behind the table was a small bookcase. The floor in the kitchen was of bare floorboards, which we found hard to keep clean and dust free, especially after we started carrying peat bags to the storage cupboard.

There were two windows in the kitchen which overlooked the back garden, but none of the windows were double-glazed and there was huge amount of condensation which collected on the windows and ran down the walls, creating a constant problem of mould.

The rayburn was for solid fuel only and had one small main oven, and also a very small warming oven, which we never used as it never got warm enough. The was no central heating from the rayburn, but it did heat the water tank.

Opposite the kitchen was another room which we called the 'sitting room' as it had the big arm chairs, an old Victorian oak dresser, a blanket chest and one large bookcase which held some of our fathers less valuable books. For a long time this was the only room where there was a rug on the floor, but we didn't use much as it was incredibly cold. The fireplace was small for the size of the room, but our father decided to put the large blanket chest in front of the fireplace, clearly having no intention that it would be used as a source of warmth.

The winding wooden staircase led up to four bedrooms. The first on the left, situated above the sitting room was the bedroom I shared with my sister. It had just one window of single glazing, no curtains, bare floorboards, one chest of drawers, a very small fireplace whose only use was to blow gales into the room down the chimney. Opposite my room was the bedroom above the kitchen and which had the airing cupboard in it. If we had visitors, this was the bedroom they were given, but it was regularly used by the two oldest siblings. Along the long landing of bare floorboards and empty walls was a small room which was used as a 'box-room' for storing stuff, and beyond that at the very end of the property was our fathers bedroom/study – as far from the kitchen as was possible.

The ceilings in the house were high and the rooms very sparsely furnished which added to the feeling of space but also coldness, and the cold was something else!

When the wind blew in every crevice of the house, through the windows, under the doors, along the floor, through the keyholes, round every corner, it was cold. The wind was cold and every draught was equally cold.

No matter how many clothes one put on, that draught got through and chilled 'right to the bone' and not infrequently it was so cold that the ice inside the upstairs windows refused to melt all day and the air was thick with moisture from our breath. I enjoyed making patterns on the ice on the windows with my breath, it was a cold but relaxing pastime.

In the long dark winters, we didn't have enough to do to keep us active and moving, so the cold dampness was able to penetrate, making it hard for us to move around and function properly.

The only heating in the house was the solid fuel rayburn in the kitchen, but that needed fuel and our father didn't buy enough fuel to burn in the rayburn continuously.

At the bottom of the staircase, there was a door which separated the main habitable rooms from the old and disused part of the house.

Behind the door was a dark and small passageway which eventually opened into quite a large room with an old fireplace which was definitely big enough to heat the whole back area. The window in this room was much more modern than the rest of the house and much lower towards the ground. There were thick wooden work benches against two of the walls. It was here we kept the garden and DIY tools.

The whole of this section of the house was always very cold, damp, dusty, and full of cobwebs, woodlice and other creepies. I did occasionally tidy up the area, and put the working tools in neat order, though it reminded me of the basement where we witnessed our brother's punishment, being similarly dusty, damp and dismal.

I always felt that at one time this part of the house had a life of its own and often wondered what that life was.

The landscape around the house was not mountainous but rather more flat and windswept with hardly any trees to break the force of the winds. Beautiful in it's own right, but the harsher climate with its long dark cold winters made it a tough place to live.

How was I going to settle into this new place? I was getting older with ever changing needs.

Playing outside was no longer an option for me. I had grown up too fast in the past two years.

Our tutor returned to stay with us for a short time, not long after we arrived and my emotions opened up to her, making sure that she was looked after as best I could. She had taken a much needed rest from her duties with us, and was making arrangements to move on with her own life. She had decided what her priorities were and was happy to follow them through.

Our belongings from storage arrived a few weeks after we did and we were glad to see everything again, and thoroughly enjoyed the luxury of having our own things to do.

I had learned to knit during our time in Wales and had been able to complete my first full sized cardigan for myself. Unfortunately the yarn I had been given to use was coloured in variegated shades of pink, which when my father saw, although he was impressed with my efforts and skills he forbade me to wear – it was the anathema pink!

Knitting was now something which we were encouraged to do everyday and soon it became part of our daily routine, and we all became very accomplished in all levels, including intricate lace work, fair isle coloured yolks and aran cables.

My father decided that I should be given the job of digging the overgrown garden. I was glad to be given something specific to do, which would keep me occupied for many days.

Hour after hour and day after day I spent digging the garden, which turned out to be a very a slow process due to the enormous number of stones I lifted with every forkful of earth, the amount of stones making every lift very heavy and picking them out interrupted the flow of work.

But I revelled in the wind blowing all around me, bashing into my face and forcing the blood to the surface, while I talked endlessly to myself, with the wind carrying my words to no-one.

Although working outside was hard work and could be very tiring, I still loved being outside, being in a place of peace by myself, a place of no competition, no oppressive feeling of being trained to please our father which was getting almost an impossibility now.

No one really wanted to be out in the cold as much as I did, being bundled up with so many clothes that it was almost impossible to bend over and pick up the stones and weeds, and wearing a hat which threatened to blow off in every gust of wind, or to fall off every time I bent over, and also wearing a skirt which blew this way and that way and every which way, no matter how much time I spent smoothing it down.

Over the years we did cultivate the garden and did grow a few things, but on the whole the exercise bore little fruit and was later abandoned on our fathers' instructions, but for now it was my haven.

Our tutor always kept in touch with us when she was away and we engaged in a detailed correspondence with her during her absences. She had moved away overseas, but had left all her furniture, books and papers with us, as she maintained regular visits, remaining loyal to our cause to the very end.

We continued to learn English grammar, composition and spelling in the form of letters which were read by our father before each posting, and were re-written if found with too many mistakes.

In one of the disused rooms at the back of the house, during one of my many rummages, I found some old school workbooks, which were copy books for learning how to write copperplate. I knew that my writing was absolutely appalling for my age, so I set about filling in these copy-books. I spent hours in my cold bedroom, too shy to let anyone know I was teaching myself to write at aged 13! I went over line after line, and then copied underneath the written line, so by the time I had completed all the empty books, and practised writing the alphabet many times, I had mastered a fairly decent hand and was finally satisfied with my ability to master a good style of copperplate.

The reception we received in the church by some of the congregation was very tentative and reserved.

We heard a lot of talking in the pews behind us, conjecturing how we spent our days, where our money came from, and what our father's line of work was.

It was totally unthinkable to them that he had no job at all!

We were used to it, but to others who had worked all their lives to make a living it was completely out of their comprehension.

We were very amused when the chattering continued on the lines of our father being connected somehow with the BBC!

Chinese whispers alright!

The chat then became direct questioning.

"What's been doing the week?".

As unused to colloquial speech as we were, we took this question personally and felt it was aimed at us, by those who disagreed with the choice of lifestyle we were living.

Again we were taking the flak for something we had no control over.

What had we done that week?

It wasn't such a bad question.

But it was a very loaded question.

We spent many hours knitting, sewing and embroidering all to a very high standard, making our own jumpers and cardigans, and also making gifts for friends. No expense was spared in using the best yarn and materials, that is until money ran out.

How could we tell those who asked "what you doin this week?" that we spent the wet, windy week knitting and writing letters?

That's what old grannies did!

They probably did more than that themselves, and they were retired school teachers or nurses or farmers wives, and were real grannies.

I hated being so odd and having a life which no-one seemed to understand.

I wasn't proud of our lifestyle at all, in fact I was embarrassed by it, and as time passed and I grew older, I knew in my own mind, that we weren't living up to our full potential at all.

I wanted to have a warm home, have an education with prospects, have a father who had a 'job' and who was not the talk of whisperers.

We had no idea how a 'normal' teenager would have answered the question we were regularly asked, other than to say they had 'been to school', but in all probability they wouldn't have been asked in the first place.

Nevertheless we had been asked, in what we felt was an attempt to make us feel uncomfortable.

We didn't see ourselves as children, but as young woman who were in apprenticeship for being housekeepers, wives and mothers, in keeping with the directions in the Bible.

If only those critics read Titus chapter 2!

We were however, welcomed into the church by many, and attended many services and missionary talks during the first few months. In fact, it seemed like it was a welcome change for them to have a family of young people attending services in an otherwise ageing congregation.

# Chapter Twelve

I so wanted to learn maths.

I had loved maths at school and knew that my maths knowledge was not keeping up with my age. I was now 14 years and knew only addition, subtraction and very simply multiplication and division. Long division and multiplication with more than two numbers, fractions and decimals was something I wanted to learn. I also wanted to be much more fluent in the multiplication tables, which I couldn't do with any confidence, speed or accuracy.

My sister asked our brother for a book on maths which we could learn from and together, she and I made our way through the thick book of equations.

It was a brilliant book which was very good at explaining each step of any new equation, and so with a lot of hard work and going through it meticulously on our own, we finally had a fair grasp of basic maths.

If our father inadvertently found us learning maths while going through the text book, he would show his disapproval by giving us his characteristic heavy frown, and say "haven't you got anything better to do?" so we restricted our book learning to the mornings, before he got up and found us working through them.

After we got as far as we could in the maths, I took up Pitman's shorthand which I thoroughly enjoyed and became proficient in. Our tutor had learned it when she was young and she was quite happy to help me however she could, often reading to me so I could practice from dictation, she would also read back what I had written, and I would read what she would write, and when she was away we would often insert shorthand sentences in our letters to each other. Although I thoroughly enjoyed learning shorthand, the purpose of doing so was not clear, and the only use I would really have for it, was taking sermon notes, or writing my own diary which I didn't want anyone else to read.

Our father didn't overtly tell us not to learn maths or shorthand, but he had a way of being so discouraging about it, that we made sure we kept it well out of sight.

The long evening's of our father's readings resumed, and I continued to listen for the twelve years I was there, and from which we had had a much needed break during our stay in Wales, the sale of our home and the move here.

These readings now included books not only from our father's large personal collection but also from some taken from the Council library.

Books such as those written by Alexandr Solzhenitsyn and other works on Communist Russia, political or christian. Also we heard extensively about the persecution of Russian christians under communist leaders and

Aida Skipnikova was much in our prayers as we learned about her suffering.

This brave young woman had suffered so much for the sake of her faith and we hoped and prayed that her contacts in the West would eventually lead to her being released.

My young and active imagination took on the idea that we might one day, face the Bible becoming illegal in our country, just as Aida had, and so with great commitment I decided to learn by heart as much of the Bible as I possible could and so during the many hours digging in the garden I set about learning many chapters and verses.

Other subjects which he covered were, global and international financial banking and this brought out the huge subject of conspiracies – who really owned what?

"Who really pulls the puppet strings?" our father got into the habit of asking, and applied this thought and question to every other subject as well.

Hearing so much about conspiracy as a teenager was very unsettling as it left me with the very distinct impression that no-one could be trusted in the outside world and that nothing was as it seemed, but this served at the time, to cement a deeper commitment to my family and faith as being the ones who had the right understanding of the world and it's events.

Another author we became very familiar with was the Danish theologian and philosopher Soren Kierkegaard, and many of his works were read to us.

In fact, many years later I found a quote from his writings which I had written in my notebook, and which has been profoundly helpful to me - "the function of prayer is not to influence God, but rather to change the nature of the one who prays".

Another subject of importance to our father at the time and which we had several days of prayer and fasting over, was the introduction of fluoride into the supply of mains water. He read about the subject himself, sifted out what to read to us and came to the understanding that he needed to object strongly on two accounts – it was enforcing medication which he believed to be illegal, and the substance itself was highly poisonous. This led him to look into further alleged conspiracy theories, about drug companies making money out of medications and it being in their interest to keep a certain amount of illness going, in order to make money from their manufactured medications.

We were introduced to Max Gerson's book "A cancer therapy" (1958) which documents his success with treating advanced cancers. Our father read this rather medically intense book full of documentation to us, and although I didn't understand a lot, I did get the idea that cancer had been cured, even advanced cancers with a change of diet, and that the 'cure' had been suppressed by US Government.

The American Civil war became a matter of great interest and we listened to many long and intricate accounts of the issues and battles involved, including Robert E Lee, and Stonewall Jackson. I got very lost trying to follow all the details of the battle scenes, read in a rather monotonous voice for too many hours to concentrate properly, but I did get some understanding of the level and cost of the conflict.

The founding of the US by the Pilgrim Fathers was also a point of interest and well covered by his reading.

"History, World Finance, Medical Ethics, Exploration and Travel" were interspersed with theology and Church History.

We learned about the Scottish Covenanters, the Highland Clearances, the English Civil War, the Great Awakening (George Whitefield), and many more church events.

Many fine points of theology were thrashed out, hymns versus psalms, infant versus adult baptism, church government and the many aspects of differing views within "Christendom" to use our father's favourite term. Every nuance of theology was laboured over.

He also read about missionary adventures which really captivated my imagination, and which I actually did enjoy listening to.

We never asked for a particular subject to be read to us, but listened to whatever book he decided to read and absorbed from it whatever we could. Some were very much more interesting than others, and some were extremely difficult to follow.

We didn't just sit passively listening to our father reading, after food was finished and he began to read, we would each resume our own knitting project and continue working on it till he finished reading. Many a garment was made to the hum of our father's voice.

During the meal we were very conscious of our father's unnoticeable attention on us. He had a way of knowing exactly what we were doing without looking at us directly. He knew if we didn't hold our cutlery properly, made too much noise eating, put elbows on the table, took too much food onto our fork at one time, or simply didn't sit quite right. Our every movement was silently scrutinised.

Sometimes our father would start to read to us immediately after we had washed the supper dishes, and we would settle down and do our handiwork as he read, other times he would start to read before the table was cleared of the empty and dirty dishes.

Occasionally our anxiety about sitting for hours with the dirty supper dishes in front of us would be eased, and we would be allowed to wash up while he was reading, but it had to be done as quietly as humanly possible, preferably without any noise at all. What mattered most of all to him, was that he wanted to continue to read and we had to respect that at all costs.

Given that the washing up had to be done in water which was boiled in the kettle first, it was no easy task at all. Taking the lid off the kettle, filling it with water, putting the lid back on and boiling the water in the kettle, then emptying the water into a basin without making any noise at all was quite a challenge.

Endeavouring to wash up in silence meant that the dishes, and not just the person doing the dishes, could not make any noise, the crockery could not be knocked, slipped or dropped, it had to be stacked on one side of the sink ready for washing, then unstacked to go into the water with the utmost precision and care, scrubbed with a brush, then placed on the draining board. It could take a very long time indeed depending on how many dishes or saucepans there were, but it was preferable to forming the bad habit of being comfortable with waking up to a load of dirty dishes first thing in the morning.

Sometimes he would read well after midnight, and when he stopped reading his chosen book, he would then insist that we would conclude the evening with family worship, no matter what time it was.

Family worship was very much according to his dictate. There was a time when we would be asked to read in turn passages of the Bible chapter which was scheduled to be read that day, and when we could choose to sing as many psalms as we wanted to, or there were times he would take the worship entirely by himself, and he might restrict the singing to one psalm or not, as per his choice.

Normally one passage from the Old Testament would be read followed by one from the New Testament, sometimes we were asked if we had any questions relating to the passage read, which if we did, we discovered that an answer could make the whole 'worship' last much longer.

Family worship would inevitable conclude with prayer, which was generally very long and the pitch of his voice would be different from his normal one. He spoke very slowly and deliberately, as if he was afraid to speak to God. He would go into a hushed vibrating tone which made my hairs stand on end.

For the family worship we now always wore our headscarves even in the home, and some of these were expensive large silk ones with bold patterns, which he has chosen and bought for us. My favourite one was made of soft wool as it was not only warm, but didn't make a noise in my ear when I moved my jaw.

These headscarves became almost as important to us as our bibles.

# Chapter Thirteen

Shortly after our move, our father visited America and had returned with an enthusiasm for the country and the civil liberties enjoyed there.

He was very taken by the Amish community, and although he appreciated much of what they valued and held onto, he thought that in many ways they were unnecessarily primitive and legalistic in their practical life. He liked the fact that the United States had room and tolerance for them to enable them to live according to their conscience, something which he hadn't been allowed to do in peace in Britain.

From that visit on, everything American was better and he constantly criticised all things British. America had become his dream and one day we would emigrate to and settle in America, the 'Promised land of milk and honey'. He made another visit there the following year and that really cemented his dream to take us all there – sometime.

Though our father or tutor never informed about issues regarding money, we were made acutely aware of matters of income by the comments we heard at church, and therefore we were left to make the assumption that our father had funded these two trips abroad with the money from the sale of our previous home.

In time we learned that if we wanted the rayburn lit more often than once or twice a week, then we needed to get our own supply of peat like the locals used and not rely on our father to provide fuel. Peat supply was free for the cutting, so after making enquiries and getting instructions from some locals, we started cutting our own supply.

Cutting, drying and collecting peat was seasonal work and had to be done when the moorland had had some time to dry out in the early summer, but when there was still enough summer left to let the peat dry outside on the moor before bringing it home and stacking it up for the winter.

Some peat banks would be miles away from the dwelling which they supplied peat for, but the bank we used was only about a mile from our house and we would often walk there carrying the tools we would need, our garden spade, garden fork and the peat-shield, which was a tool specially designed for the sole purpose of cutting peat.

On the peat moor we would cut off the top layer of heather with a garden spade, which exposed the peat layer lying underneath. The peat looked a bit like dark moist chocolate cake. This 'cake' was cut into very precise pieces by a 'peat shield' and these were laid out to dry on the heather moorland. If there was more than one person working, then one person would dig out the peat with the peat shield, and the other person would take the cut pieces from the digger, and lay them spaced out on the heather. Having enough workers to keep pace with the person cutting the peat, made the whole job much quicker which was really helpful, as enough peat had to be cut for the whole year, in a very short window of time. A good peat bank would have peat going down as far as 6-10 feet, and digging at this level made lifting the wet pieces to the surface very hard physical work, but ours went down about 5-6 ft which was deep enough for me being of short statue.

When peat blocks are dried they are extremely solid and can have ragged and tough edges, but ours tended to be crumbly, so we had to be put most of our supply into old fertilizer bags to bring home and store.

Bagging up the peat was very back-breaking work. First one had to pick up all the pieces from the ground bending over, put them into bags, and then the bags onto the trailer to be unloaded at home.

As novices and only teenagers this was hard work for us and our peat bank had very poor quality peat, very crumbly, very difficult to stack, turn and dry, and which either burned very quickly or didn't burn at all.

It was very disheartening and it often felt as though we put more heat into getting the peat, than we ever got out from burning it.

By his obvious absence it became clear to us that our father didn't like physical work or getting dirty. Only very occasionally would he help to bring the bags home after borrowing a tractor to load them up.

Returning home to no hot water and a meagre supper of another omelette and rice, after a day of being out on the moor and in the dirt, did nothing to inspire my good will and forbearance.

The notion of being used would sometimes cross my mind as I laboured hard to help provide for us. As time went on it seemed as if we were living a self-perpetuating existence and all I was doing was being used to continue it. Something didn't sit quite right, but I pushed such thoughts into the back of my mind. "Ours was not to question why, but to comply", we were women (female) and women had to be submissive to their god-given moral headship.

When other work wasn't possible, I often spent the time collecting wood for the fire, or sawing huge logs of timber. Although it was hard work, I relished using my otherwise redundant muscles and it gave me purpose during the day. It was something useful to do.

Sitting still on the wooden dinning chairs and listening to hours of reading after doing a lot of outside manual labour I found very difficult and also being out in the strong fresh air for hours tended to make one feel very sleepy when returning back into the warmth.

I wasn't able to relax in a warm bath after working outside, as there wasn't a constant supply of hot water and having a bath was limited to a rota system and was only possible to have a bath on the days that the rayburn was lit and heated the water, and then only if there was enough hot water left in the tank after all the clothes washing was done.

And there were times when I thought that my father's expectation of me physically was rather unreasonable.

One of the things I found very hard was after having done a hard days work no matter how heavy, dirty, difficult, tiring, smelly and tough it was, and then to be the epitome of the impeccable, educated 'lady of the manor' in deportment and manners in the evening, having to wear the same work clothes and not be able to wash properly and relax my hard-worked muscles. In this area, I really felt my sisters had the advantage, as more of my time was spent in physical labour than theirs.

After a year or so of moving into our home we noticed that things started to get scarce, that the shopping supply brought home was smaller and smaller, also our supply of knitting yarn was getting limited, and supplies like toilet paper was no longer bought and we started cutting up the paper bags taken from the supermarket into little squares and used these instead - not at all a comfortable substitute for toilet paper.

There were times when our electricity would be cut off without warning, when we were in the middle of doing absolutely anything, and be plunged into immediate darkness mid sentence, mid cooking, reading books or knitting patterns, or we would find out there was no longer a supply of electricity when we tried to put a light on, or needed to boil the kettle.

The electricity wouldn't be cut off due to a power failure, or because of bad weather, or the frequent gales in our area, but was cut off because the bill hadn't been paid.

During the times there was no electricity we had the rayburn for cooking and for any hot water needed for drinking, we would often have to make an extra effort to heat the rayburn with our meagre and inefficient fuel, or we would use the one paraffin stove we had but which was designed for heating only, and definitely not for putting any sort of saucepan on. It was a real challenge to cook on this stove, and trying to heat a pan full of water on it gave another dimension to time.

We did have a paraffin lamp for light, which we were able to use when there was a sufficient supply of paraffin. We would use what candles we had and try to make them last as long as we possible could, not knowing how long that needed to be.

After days, sometimes weeks without electricity it would be reconnected as mysteriously as it went off, and we would bask in the luxury of lights and have a respite from the trials of existing with the very minimal of equipment.

There was however, one comfort which we never did without whatever our difficulties, and that was our hot-water bottle, at least one each, which were not only essential in the unheated bedrooms and cold beds, but were also our little bits of personal comfort.

Even though our father hadn't long come back from a long trip to America, I thought he hadn't looked after affairs at home where we were, though he had asked John to keep an eye on us. I tried to understand how he was able to make such decisions, and how did he justify them, but concluded it was too difficult and also probably not meant for me to understand. I was only a child and most probably not in possession of all the facts.

# Chapter Fourteen

John was an elder in the church we attended, and had a croft about three miles from our home, and apparently we owed John a favour as he was responsible for us staying in the church house at no cost to us.

So when John arrived at the front door one day and asked if we could help him with harvesting his corn, our father didn't hesitate to agree.

During the couple of weeks it took us to complete the harvest work, our needs were very well supplied in John's home, where there was a constant supply food and warmth which was such a luxury for us.

Breakfast was served mid-morning after a couple hours work, and was the most delicious meal of sausages, bacon, toast, ketchup, and tea with milk and sugar.

A whole plateful of hot food in morning!

Then there were cakes and tea served mid-afternoon.

Heavenly cakes - all sorts of different cakes and biscuits which in our house would be classed as 'cheap junk food' were so delicious. Supper would then eaten at about 6.00pm and consist of something like a casserole, stew or 'tatties and mince'.

The warmth that hit me when coming in from the wind into a small kitchen heated by an effective rayburn was absolute bliss.

If this was how other people lived, I liked it.

John's croft was very small of just a few acres, a hundred sheep and a couple of cows. He still used the old fashioned method of cutting the corn with a binder. After being cut with the binder, the corn was stood out to dry in the fields before a combine harvester would be hired for a day and thrash out the crop, separating the straw stalks from the corn heads.

Once the corn was cut in the field, it was put into bundles which were tied in the middle and these are bundles are called sheafs, and these sheafs needed to be stood up on the stalk end, and six sheafs together would make a stook. The stooks would dry for a week or two then be gathered up onto a trailer and built into a rick, which is how the harvest is stored before being thrashed by the combine harvester and then used for winter bedding and fodder for the animals.

Building the stooks needed to done carefully, and they had to face the best way for the wind to dry the corn heads out, and it had to stand on its own and be strong enough to stand against the strong natural winds, so common in that area.

When the stooks were dry enough to build into a rick, we were asked to help again and were happy to do so.

I loved being on the trailer handing the sheaves to John who was building the rick. We worked in perfect silent harmony as I threw the sheaves in the correct direction to him turning them on my pitch fork if necessary, while he laid them down in a very specific way and built the rick. As he moved his position on the rick, I had to change the direction I threw the sheaf to him. We worked well as a team, and there was a mutual understanding about what we were doing which was a great feeling for me, as I knew I was doing something not just right but also doing it well.

John really appreciated the ease with which we worked together. As his rick was growing higher and higher, my trailer load of sheafs was getting lower and lower, the distance I had to throw a sheaf up to him became greater, which made lifting and throwing harder, but this was accompanied with a sense of great satisfaction as it meant the work was being done and coming to a satisfactory end.

A land-worker knows only too well the immense sense of relief when the years' harvest is brought home safe and dry, and we were aiming towards this.

We worked hard and long for the short time the weather permitted the harvest to be done. I enjoyed every moment, being in the freedom of the fields, having a purpose to the day, helping someone who in turn helped others. I needed those care-free days of not being watched and judged and never feeling good-enough – the feeling I had everyday at home.

Eventually John started to ask for help with different jobs on his croft all year round, and I would be the one who would normally go and help him out from shearing sheep, paring the sheeps hoofs, sometimes dipping the sheep or even mowing the church yard grass.

John enjoyed life and we had some great times together. He had learned to make the most of his physical handicap which had not stopped him earning a living off the land, building his own house or being an accomplished carpenter.

Some of the work we did together wasn't easy, but we always managed to complete what he had set out to do, sometimes battling the rough wind, laughing in the rain, or braving the ice.

No matter what job we did we always enjoyed it and had many conversations on all sorts of topics. His was a friendship which made a big difference to me during those rather austere and bleak years.

While working in John's field the second year we helped him with his corn harvest, I was exposed to a side of my father which I hadn't seen before and which changed my view of him as the perfect father who everyone should look up to. He showed a human side of himself which tainted the notion I had of him.

He was driving the tractor and the tractor needed to be attached to the trailer. He reversed the tractor towards the trailer and I was holding the iron pin which locks the two together by matching up the holes in each part, the pin then slides through the holes which are in both machines and secures them both together.

He told me to "put the pin in" but I could see that the holes were not aligned properly so the pin wouldn't slide in properly.

He repeated "put the pin in".

I didn't know how to 'put the pin in' as the holes were not together for the pin to be 'put in'.

He raised his voice in frustration and just repeated "put the pin in".

Again he said "put the pin in".

I could feel the tears whelming up as I simply didn't know how to do what I was being told to do, and having my father shout at me for not obeying because I didn't understand, was humiliating for me. Needless to say I got the 'silent' treatment for many a day after that. If only he explained what he wanted rather than just repeated himself. If only he had made complying with him easier. I decided he was definitely not suited to working in the fields and that I was happy to be left working without him.

In fact, I was beginning to be happier in his absence.

John had a great sense of humour which I appreciated and which was a relief from the intensity at home, where we had taken the words of the bible literally- Matthew 12:26 "I say unto you, That every idle word that men shall speak, they shall give account thereof in the day of judgement".

The day of judgement became a very real thing, an event which will definitely take place, where we shall stand before God and give an account of our lives and actions. So we became very careful what we said, making sure that we said as little as possible and nothing unnecessary.

John's family had the same church membership, faith and beliefs as we did, but they lived their lives rather differently to us, and I felt their way of life and attitude was kinder and more humane.

But then, we were taught that we had a purer form of thought and behaviour, we were the obedient ones, the uncompromised ones, who 'suffered for righteousness' sake' because of our uncompromising obedience, and that it was the state of 'Christendom' which was the cause of our situation, our poverty and distress, and it was 'Christendom' that didn't understand or appreciate our father's position. It was as though we had an underlying attitude that if one wasn't suffering for following Christ, then one wasn't following Christ as one should.

Our father made it quite clear that our situation was always the responsibility of something or someone outside of us. "If a ruler harken to lies, all his servants are wicked" and our 'ruler' (the government) had 'harkened' to lies, so any one employed by the government was compromised. This put almost everyone we knew in a dubious category, being either teachers, nurses or other government employees, and I found this to be a very sad position to take and one which I was unable to really embrace.

This idea and his steadfast commitment to it, meant that no government money could be received in our house either, no unemployment benefit for those of us who were now of age, or for our father.

As a young person in this situation, I didn't try and analyse things too much - that happened a lot later, now I accepted things as they were, tried to make the most of any given circumstance and be obedient.

It took a lot of energy just to live, survive and be alive.

I didn't want any more conflict.

# Chapter Fifteen

Our father used words to teach us, and his frown to govern us.

That deliberate, disturbing and painfully persistent frown was deep under his heavy eyebrows.

With it he expressed displeasure, intolerance and judgement, with the desired effect of making me intensely intimidated, guilty and worried, and was often accompanied by a physical turning away, giving the hidden and implied message that he didn't like something.

He never honoured me with an explanation as to exactly what might have caused his disapproval. That was something which I had to guess, and guessing meant that there was a possibility of getting it wrong and if I did get it wrong, the whole process would start all over again.

I noticed he started exhibiting this behaviour towards my oldest sister, the one who had been given the responsibility of us after our tutor had left so suddenly. She was only sixteen at the time she had to take charge of her younger sisters, having had no preparation for the task, and had done so without complaining, so why he started to pelt down this heavy disapproving frown and turn away from her, while she was doing her duties and chores, neither she nor any of her sisters knew. Our father appeared to have turned almost overnight and now would just give her that awful frown, no words, just a devastating look which said so much without uttering a single word. I knew this was making her feel worthless, unloved, disliked, unvalued and unwanted which lead to her becoming reclusive and depressed. I felt very much for her and wished I could have done something to ease her sadness.

A few months later and I too became the recipient of those awful frowns, every day, all day, and day after day. I desperately tried to work out what I had done to displease him so much that he could turn so deliberately.

I would be doing something simple like walk into the room and he would give his signature look of disapproval as though I was far beneath him and then he would turn away, making it quite clear by his body language that it was absolutely and completely unacceptable to communicate with him.

He had spoken with his look and that should have been enough for us to understand the message that he was trying to convey.

During supper he made the atmosphere particularly uncomfortable and intense for me, by giving me that soul-destroying look of intolerance. I wondered if it was the way I sat, ate, held things, spoke, didn't speak, looked, or didn't look. He was determined that I wouldn't find out from his lips whatever it was that caused him to look at me like he did.

When I would be told supper was ready, a tight ball would rise in my stomach as my nervous tension increased knowing what I was about to go through at the table, and for a reason I simply couldn't fathom out, no matter how hard I tried, It was paramount to our very being, the reason for our existence to please the moral headship given to us, and I was quite clearly not doing that.

The guilt on me was heavy.

It all became exhausting as I tried to find a reason for his displeasure, so that I could correct whatever it was that mattered so much to him. I never stopped trying for as long as I was with him, and I never did find out.

He perpetuated his authoritarian air of being unapproachable, untouchable and without question the master of his family.

Every day I lived under the burden of thinking I had done something wrong, distasteful, unattractive, uneducated and every day the hurt and guilt grew and grew. Every day I was met with more frowns.

It was the deliberate turning away which added insult to injury. He would turn away from one daughter with an inexplicable look of destain, to another daughter with a look of pure pleasure and satisfaction with no given reason. I hadn't done anything to displease him that I could think of, so I had to conclude that maybe it was just me as me he simply didn't like.

All I could do was to accept it and make the best of life that I could, after all he was my father and the only parent I had known for many years, and I had to believe, that in his own way he did love his children.

One day I raised my question very carefully to him about the right of having a favoured child, making sure I made no reference to what I was really feeling and thinking, and careful not to make a personal challenge, keeping my question to a point of theology.

He justified his behaviour by saying that there are many examples in the Old Testament of fathers having favoured children.

So I was silenced by the Bible.

By this time I had been the best part of seven years under his teaching and had been finely instructed about the place of women. It had been instilled into me for years to do as I was told, that women must do as their head (male authority) says. His word was the will of God in our lives, as he was the god-appointed authority over us. To disobey him was tantamount to disobeying God.

He had the ability to make everything he said sound Biblical, so believable, so upright, so unquestionable, so god-given and pure, coming only from a place of righteousness and willingness to please and obey God.

As far back as I could remember our father didn't have paid work and we could only guess where our livelihood came from. We knew that we were supported in part by our tutor and for a while by the sale of the previous family home. Our tutor was now living away and although she sent things to us from time to time, it didn't stop the downward spiral of physical poverty.

We could always hear him make his approach to the kitchen for his breakfast every day, by hearing his slippers against the floorboards.

Flop - flop - flop - flop as he came down the landing, his footsteps making echoes which bounced off the empty walls.

Flip - flip - flip as he descended the stairs.

It was a noise I learned over the years to dislike very much, and even dread.

As soon as we heard him approaching we scuppered like frighted rodents, from the warmth of the kitchen – the only warm room in the house, gather up any 'stuff' we were doing, books, knitting, or pen and paper and we would scatter ourselves round the house, sometimes going to our own bedrooms or to the cold 'sitting room' no matter what time of year it was or how cold it was in the rest of the house, we never stayed in the kitchen. We gave him the privacy to wake up, read his bible and drink his coffee in the peace of his own company.

He would normally sit for an hour or two in the kitchen having his breakfast reading, always the Book of Proverbs, and drinking copious amounts of coffee.

Often in the winter he would get up very late – like just as day light was giving way to dust, and other times he would come down in the morning. We would never know when, but our ears were tuned for that flip-flop noise and we would be ready for him to make his appearance.

We used the word 'banished' to describe our time out of the kitchen when he was the sole occupier, and we would rush back into the warmth as soon as he returned to his own room.

Occasionally one of us would have to stay in the kitchen to make bread or stoke the fire in the rayburn, but that was done as quietly and therefore slowly as possible.

This routine only added to the feeling that he was in reality unapproachable, despite the theology and teachings on subjects such as christian unity, working together, fatherhood and fellowship.

But we accepted the way things were in the home and his authority over us.

I believed that the more I prayed the better I would become, the more holy, more Christlike, more refined by grace, so I formed a habit of taking a prayer time at 4.00pm every day. I would stop whatever I was doing and go into 'my space' – the cupboard under the back staircase, I had chosen as my place of devotion.

An hour-and-a-half spent kneeling, cramped into a small cupboard made it hard for me to stand up and stretch out my cramped and cold joints as I adjusted my eyes to the light.

Each day without fail I would go into the cupboard, the only exception being the day the kitchen was fully occupied with all hands on deck to do the weeks' washing and bread-making, and try to keep the sluggish rayburn burning to provide the hot water for the washing and a hot oven to bake the bread.

There in this cupboard I committed in prayer my whole life to God, all my aspirations, hopes, dreams and desires and my spirit to obedience and a life pleasing to God, I confessed all my known and unknown sins of commission and omission and prayed for all those I knew.

Here in childlike, deep sincerity and honesty I poured out my very soul.

It was here that I built dreams of my future life.

I became obsessed with this ritual and it become as important to me as life.

Initially I don't think anyone noticed I had disappeared for a long time as it was quite normal to be left to spend time out on our own, and unless we were required in the kitchen there was no timetable to adhere to, and we were free to do as we pleased.

One day as I was leaving the kitchen to go to 'my space', my oldest sister interrupted me going out and asked me to help her in the kitchen.

Next thing I knew, she kept me busy 'helping' and 'inventing' jobs which she needed help with, and all I could think of was my 'appointment' with God and essential prayer time.

I was very upset that I couldn't make my sacred time that day.

The next day the same thing happened, and the next.

I struggled with my obsession being taken from me with no explanation or understanding on my part.

I quietly acknowledge to myself, that my sister had started to worry about my well-being – for a whatever reason she could see which I couldn't, and had decided that my habit of long, cramped and cold prayer times needed to come to an end.

However misguided I was in my sense of obligation to a God of mercy, it was not taken into consideration or treated with any respect by those caring for me, and I certainly felt it, every bit of it. It felt like a violation of my conscience, my very soul by another had taken place. I once again had to accept that I had 'no mind, no rights, no feelings'.

I was now fifteen and steeped into the spiritual and religious life we knew.

I had all but forgotten what life was like before I was seven.

One of the local congregations held psalm-singing rehearsals with a view to holding an evening of singing and we quite willingly joined these rehearsals and in fact we rather enjoyed them, and were heavily relied on as the only young voices in the group. Our father however, was slightly reluctant for us to attend but allowed us to nevertheless.

On the evening the performance was held, we waited for our father to finish supper and take us to the church. He didn't take us or tell us what he had decided. After all, if we waited long enough his decision would become quite clear. We just watched the clock go past the hour the performance started.

We never arrived.

We worried about how we had let the evening performance down.

Deja vu.

We just didn't turn up when people were relying on us just like the day so long before when we didn't go to the Sunday School outing.

Deja vu the embarrassment of explaining the next time we saw members of the church, why we had let everyone down at the last minute and why our father was so unapproachable that no one had the courage to ask him why he chose to be so unsociable.

I was now sixteen not eight years old, with teenage frustration in full swing and I started to feel the embarrassment very keenly and personally. As a young child one can hide behind ones' parents, but one is normally expected to have a 'say' in things as one gets older, but our father didn't comply with the 'norm' and our standing was much the same with him at sixteen as it was at eight, based on his understanding of the 'moral' order of headship, obedience and submission.

# Chapter Sixteen

'Fill it in and send it off" John said with a twinkle in his eye handing me a form for a provisional driving licence.

I was embarrassed by his generosity but also had a bit of worry knowing the difficult position 'filling it and sending it off' would inevitable put me in with my family.

I was the youngest, but the first to be offered a driving licence!

How would my sisters react and above all, would I be allowed to 'send it off' by the ultimate voice of authority?

I didn't have the heart to say anything to him, so took the form and the accompanying postal order, and set my mind to wondering how to approach this matter at home.

We owed John, as he continued to insist that our father wouldn't be charged for the use of the house, while there were others dealing with the church finances who wanted to charge him rent.

Our father was very conscious of his debt to John, and so reluctantly, he allowed me to 'send it off' and I did receive my provisional license.

This allowed John to take me out more often than just needing help on the croft.

My very first lesson was on an old wartime aerodrome where John talked me through the various switches, levers and peddles, explaining what each one did and in what order they were to be used and when, and then expected me to drive!

I had been instructed, so what more was there to learn?

His face turned into a broad smile – he knew what he was doing, he knew that he was using his humour to teach me, and he enjoyed every bit of it, especially my reaction. Having got through that set of 'instructions' John turned out to be a very good, trusting and patient teacher.

We spent many hours practising my driving going to and from the croft, or into town, and it wasn't long before I became quite a confident driver.

I had started to enjoy more and more time with John and his sister, as life at home had become harder and harder, not just the physical circumstances but also my own teenage reactions increased my inner tensions.

John aptly described me as being "like a frightened mouse, near a cat that's about to pounce".

There were 'two sides of the coin' at being the one who was always sent out to help John, on the one hand it was a welcome change going to John's and feeling that I was wanted, needed, useful, respected and talked to and to have a purpose and focus to the day, and also to enjoy the food and warmth in return for my endeavours. The 'other side of the coin' was feeling completely dispensable at home, and particularly that I was a burden and 'another mouth to feed' (as my father would say) – the last child and one too many.

I chose to concentrate on the positive side, so every time I heard footsteps coming up the garden path in a morning, followed by the ringing of the doorbell, I hoped against hope that it was my call to work, to spend the day away from the freezing house, the drafts, the hunger and the intensity of the atmosphere, but above all away from the crushing frowns and disapproving scowls which had become part of every day life and something which although caused great distress, I had come to live with.

One morning in late summer, just after I had turned 17, John fetched me to help him with the chosen task of the day - bagging peat, and he drove directly to his peat bank some few miles away from his home. It was somewhere I had never been to before with John as he didn't believe that working on the peat bank was suitable work for woman, but today he made an exception, as it was only the 'lighter' task of bagging up the peat which needed to be done. John's peat was far superior to ours and bagging it was not as difficult as bagging ours.

The sun was shining over the moor and the wind was gentle, with little clouds in the blue sky telling us that we had better get to work before they started leaving their droplets and making our work heavier. The late summer air carried its unique smell of heather and freshness and the scene before us was peaceful with no-one else in sight for as far as we could see.

Before getting out of the car, John said that he had something he wanted to say and I was eager to listen, as what he said was usually significant or interesting.

In his characteristic no nonsense way, he made a statement which I think was meant to be a question.

"I want you to be my wife".

That's not what I was expecting at all.

I was listening to my own voice saying "you should have done it years ago John".

"What, got married?"

"Yes" I replied.

He swiftly answered "Ah, yes, but I didn't meet you years ago did I?."

"No, you didn't" I said, "but you met many other woman I'm sure."

"Yes, but none nice in every way like you are." was his response.

I knew he was a lot older than me, and was really too old for this sort of thought, but couldn't bring myself to say that directly to him.

Once I had made it clear that it would be necessary for him to ask my father, we got to work for the rest of the day and little more was said on the matter.

Back at home I was still feeling the warmth from John's sentiment but decided not to tell anyone. I wanted to experience the glow of being loved, at least for now and for as long as it lasted.

I wondered what it was that John saw in me that no-one else in the family seemed to. What qualities did he see?

About a week later John visited us to discuss the matter with my father. I didn't really expect him to take it that far at all. I thought that by saying he needed to ask my father he would be put off, and not wish to cross that hurdle.

Not that I didn't like John, but considering I was now seventeen and he was at the other end of the age spectrum, I didn't take his question too seriously.

But he seemingly did.

About a week later John visited our home and spoke to my father privately in the kitchen. After he left my father didn't say a word to me about what had been discussed, but the next day I was sent away to England, to join my brother who was working there, and who was waiting for the result of his visa application to emigrate to America. Our oldest sister had gone ahead a few months earlier.

John was devastated at my departure and felt responsible for my 'banishment to England' as he described it.

We corresponded very regularly, both of us taking delight in writing and giving each other a detailed account of what we were doing. I heard about life on the croft, new calves and nursing mothers, sheeps hoofs that needed paring, little lambs born and lost in the cold or flourishing well. He in turn, read about sermons I had listened to, books I was reading, the weather in England or what I was knitting.

John's handwriting was something I had never seen, and was very touched when I did see how he had perfect cursive lettering despite the physical deformity of his curled right hand and shortened arm. I in turn, made great effort to make my letters works of art with drawings of flora on the top page and writing in my best calligraphy.

My brother read the occasional letter, as my father had instructed him to, to make sure our correspondence was within the 'moral boundaries.'

My life was now on a housing estate with all modern conveniences, and with a brother who was bringing home an income. In every way a stark contrast to what I was used to.

The hardest thing here to make the sudden adjustment to, was that there was nothing really to occupy myself with, and the reality of this hit me every day. There was no garden to dig and not many books to read, no places to go for a walk and very little knitting to do as yarn had been left in Scotland.

Out of shear boredom I would translate what books I did read into shorthand, and the shorthand sermon notes I took every Sunday I would transcribe into longhand.

Not so long after my own arrival, the rest of the family arrived from Scotland and took up residence, as our father seemed so convinced that our time had come to pack up in Scotland, close the house and head out to America, the land of Civil Liberty.

We all tried to live in this small house, certainly not designed for a family of five grown-up people who stayed in it all day long. This was a house designed for the modern working family who did little more than bed and breakfast in it.

For all the trials we had in Scotland at least there had been sufficient space in the house and plenty of space outside. Being here was a trial of a different nature, equally thrust on us and unwelcome.

The sisters who now joined us, told me that the day John found out I had been sent to England, he went to our house and confronted our father and vented his anger at what he perceived was my punishment and which was something I didn't deserve. Years of helping us out and supporting us were vented, and John had snapped at our father for the way he treated us.

Challenging our father, no matter who you were never ended well, and all John succeeded in doing was expressing the opinion he and many others held, about how we were treated and about some of our father's behaviour and views. Any challenge made to our father only resulted in him being even more determined to do his own thing. Nothing anyone said ever changed our father's thought as he believed that he was answerable to God only and to no-one else.

# Chapter Seventeen

Our father had kept in contact with some of his contacts in America from his visits and had now received an invitation to go back and to take two of his daughters with him. The fares for the girls would be paid for by the American side of the arrangement as they were asked to help with a family in need of some support.

My father left England and arrived in Washington State with two of my sisters, who had got a visitors visa for six months.

Hearing from our sisters in America in their frequent letters, I was glad to know that they were very happy and well looked after in, that they had plenty of friends and companionship and also lots of helpful things to do.

I was also very glad for the break from our father and from his nervous, worried, uptight and intense presence.

I was hopeful that maybe our life as it had been, would be approaching an end, and that our father would finally allow us to do something useful for others and use our 'god-given talents' progressing normally into womanhood.

Just maybe there was room for hope.

How would America influence him?

Our brother's emigration visa was approved in the time expected, so he needed to pack up his home and leave the country. Our father had returned from America, with no obvious way forward with his plans, so we had no option but to return to Scotland, and it was with a very heavy heart and considerable foreboding I had to return to the home I had left only a few months before, and to whatever life and future would unfold for me there. One thing I knew for certain – it would be a cold life.

I knew there wouldn't be the comfort or the breaks, which times with John had given me in the past, and I knew that my sisters being away would mean that I would have to work closer with our father in helping to keep the household running.

None of these prospects were welcoming, comfortable or encouraging.

In the cold house where everything had been packed into boxes and trunks, there was a very unsettled feeling. The house was no longer a home, but more like a camping experience with only the bare minimum of things to use.

Our two sisters returned from America after having their visa's extended by three months, making the whole of their time a full nine months away.

Going back to Scotland was heartbreaking for them as they had experienced life so differently in other families.

But now, we didn't even have the hand brush which goes with a 'dustpan and brush' set, only the dustpan part, and we needed to sweep up the constant fall of ash and dirt and peat dust from the rayburn. We asked our father if we could please stop using our hand to gather up the mess, and were told that there would be "no need for a brush on the aeroplane to America".

We thought this was quite stupid reasoning and we totally resented it. Did he ever go on his knees and try to clean the mess with his hands? Of course not!

Our father had become more and more convinced that America was the only place where he (and us) would be able to live as he wanted to live.

He had met so many families in America who were home-schooling their children, who questioned paying taxes to an 'unchristian' government, and who were ready to fight for what they believed in. He found many like-minded people which only served to increase his resolve and keep everything packed up until his dream became his reality.

Such was his conviction that it permeated everyday life with real consequences to us in trying to keep a home.

Sometimes our father made life so impossible, so difficult, so infuriatingly hard.

He would expect something of us, then make it as hard as he possible could for us to accomplish what he wanted done.

When it came to the supper table he expected us to be the ultimate epitome of an English Lady, yet was quite willing to watch us on our hands and knees struggling with dirt and ashes just before supper.

This small but memorable incident of the 'dust-pan-and-brush' made me quietly question within myself how unrealistic he was with us and how completely 'idealistic' he was with himself.

I knew there was no way John would have expected himself or his sister to do a job without proper tools.

Something was out of kilter in our home.

Although our father admired America and the newly-made friends, we couldn't help but notice that those who he admired all had jobs and did an honest day's work – perhaps that was the real reason they were prospering.

He continued to purport that the reason we were in such difficulties was the 'state of Christendom'. I started to turn a deaf ear to him when he went on about it, as I was more concerned with the practical issues of survival.

It was in the end the hunger that got to me.

That basic instinct of survival kicked in strongly.

What weight I had, I was losing rapidly.

I knew my body was giving its strength up.

I started to crave warm mutton fat.

The idea of some warm mutton fat was heavenly and I just longed for what most people would throw away.

I was hungry.

I was very hungry indeed.

This hunger took over every waking moment and I just had to find a way of getting some food.

I cycled to John's, asked if I could use his rabbit snares.

I distinctly got the feeling from John that he wasn't impressed with my request at all, but I was so fixated on getting some food, that I didn't think of how John must have felt about me asking him for help.

He wouldn't have wanted to see me in need, but neither would he have wanted to do anything to help our father perpetuate his lifestyle and I put him into a difficult position and that's maybe why his reaction was not with the warmth and enthusiasm I was used to him showing.

When real deep hunger takes hold, everything else in life fades into insignificance and that hunger makes one behave in what could be misunderstood as a selfish way, but it's only selfish in the way that is inbuilt in every person to do whatever it takes to survive.

I had reached that point and used what ingenuity, independence and imagination I had to find a solution.

After sorting out the snares with John and returning home, I traipsed the moors and fields setting the snares.

I had been shown how to skin a rabbit by our tutor years before, and so after my first catch, I set my mind to the necessary part but the one I disliked the most.

Apparently it is easier to skin an animal when it is still warm, before the fatty layer just under the skin has not hardened by cooling down but, all sentiment aside even when driven by hunger, I just couldn't skin a warm animal.

I just had to wait for the rabbits to get cold.

One evening my father surprised us all by saying that I should be sent out to catch some rabbits to feed the family.

Little did he know that my first catch was already hanging in the backroom of the old part of the house.

Although I had pre-empted his thought and found my own way to try and satisfy an overwhelming hunger, I couldn't help noticing that he chose me again. I was always being the one to do work, the dirty work, the hard work, the work least lady-like. Perhaps it was because I could be counted on to get my sleeves up and 'bring the bacon home', or maybe it was because he viewed me as an asset. I never knew but as his governance by looks and frowns continued, along with his oversensitivity to noise, I very much felt that it was me as an asset that was of value.

Day after day, morning after morning and evening after evening, I went in pursuit of rabbits, checking on the snares and bringing home those that were destined to support our life.

Often something else got them before I did – a fox or a bird of prey and I was left to care for the remaining carcases left in the snare.

Rabbits are caught in snares because they don't see the snares and jump into the hole of the snare which should be set at the right height for their head to go into on the upward thrust of their jump. This means that darkness is required to catch rabbits in snares so they don't see the snare and are able to avoid it during their evening or morning run. When the daylight hours became long enough for the snares to be seen by the rabbits the hunting season stopped and with it our supply of regular meat.

It always baffled me why our father never ate any of the rabbit meat he had suggested I went out and caught. We would mostly make stews, but he would always rather eat something else.

He was such an anomaly.

So intransigent.

# Chapter Eighteen

When the dinners of rabbit stew had to stop with the approach of summer, I had to make another plan to get food.

My next plan was more stable.

I would get some goats!

Yes, I would have goats to milk.

With the financial help of our tutor, I bought very cheaply, my first Saanen goat.

She was an older nanny who had had many kids and was a prolific milker. The lady I bought her from delivered her to us and I housed her in the otherwise empty barn which was on the periphery of our property.

My days now had more purpose, I had the care of animals to get up to in the morning.

It was still very difficult to get up in the freezing cold bedroom, but I was motivated by the love I had for Esther my nanny goat and her dependency on me.

I had the use of a field not far from the house, where Esther would go for most of the day. She was resilient to wind and rain of which there was plenty, and she didn't have a naughty streak in her, so I knew she would never try to escape.

I hated the smell of goats, it was the one drawback of keeping them.

I hated smelling of goats all day, and that smell getting right into my clothes and never going away. It was a strong musty smell, distinct and pungent.

There wasn't enough regular hot water and soap to scrub that smell away and replace it with something more bearable, pleasant and feminine which I would have loved to have been able to enjoy.

If I wanted to wash after working with the goats, I would have to either use very cold water in a very cold bathroom with a damp towel, or I would have to boil a kettle of water in the kitchen, and put it into the bathroom sink, knowing that by the time I had returned the kettle to the kitchen and got back to the bathroom, the water would be tepid at best. The coldness and dampness and mould of the bathroom was enough to discourage any habit of washing.

I was afraid of turning into an old smelly farm woman, and I hated the very thought let alone the possibility.

With good husbandry my one goat soon multiplied into several!

I had goats milk enough to drink and to make cheese and yoghurt from.

I even had enough to give to the farmer for lambs, and what was left I would sell in the local post-office store.

I was good at this! I put the work in and was rewarded well for my efforts.

In the height of season and with food Esther alone would give about 13 pints a day.

The goats were now my reality, and soon I had kids to raise, de-horn those which I wanted to keep, and take to the slaughterhouse those who had another destiny.

This work kept me outside and occupied more than I had ever been, but I was happy enough, so long as I kept in the present and didn't start to wonder where I might be in tens years, or how in this bleak place I would ever get to met someone I could possibly marry.

Marriage. The ultimate goal for woman. The one and only role I had been trained for since the age of seven.

One day our father received a letter from someone with connections in the church, asking if he knew of anywhere he could stay in the locality.

He was invited to stay with us in our home for the few days he needed to be in the area. He arrived by train and stayed with us in our poor abode and our lack of modern comforts without indicating any discomfort at all.

Many hours were spent by him and our father talking and sharing ideals, principles, theology and reading lists, as we went about our daily tasks of trying the keep the fire hot, the water hot, food cooked and the house clean.

The evening before he left to go back home, he told me that he had asked my father if he could write to me.

To me?

Yes, to me.

My reaction was mixed.

I was flattered to have been noticed, but also there was the painful reminder of what had happened when this subject had been brought up before.

I still wasn't free from a sense of guilt.

Being the youngest, one normally expects to have the older ones leave first, but here was a real possibility of me having an opportunity to change my life.

We had already learned from bitter disappointments that two of my older sisters had gone through, that our father was extremely difficult to please when it came to approving of someone for his daughters.

We also knew that he was extremely particular on every point of doctrine.

Every point had to be agreed on and we knew that that was almost an impossibility.

Having trained us for marriage for many years, it seemed to us as if he was putting up all sorts of hurdles and blocks to make sure it didn't happen.

All we wanted was the loving approval of a loving father for a loving relationship in our lives, and sooner rather than later.

So much harder to get than it was to be talked about!

I soul-searched about my motives regarding wanting to accept Jim's offer of 'corresponding with a view to a further relationship'.

Did I just want a way out of this gruesome and seemingly endless situation and would take any route offered?

How much was I really prepared to leave all decisions up to my father in this matter?

Did I have any alternative but to submit wholly to my father's wish about this.

My questioning aside we wrote copious letters and all seemed to be going well.

During his next visit shortly after, our father and Jim had talked for hours every day at the kitchen table as my sister tried desperately to get on with the chores of the day. She listened to all the theology being thrashed out and became very disturbed at the attitude of our visitor, who seemed to be completely absorbed in theology not noticing he was making the day's work so much harder by keeping our father at the table, requiring such quietness from anyone working in the kitchen, that it was almost impossible to do the necessary work.

It was strange for us to watch Jim being so confident with our father. He had no idea of our father's habit of being by himself in the kitchen for the first hours after getting up, and whilst we quickly vacated the kitchen on our father's arrival from up stairs, Jim confidently stayed in the warmth and was ready and eager to engage our father in conversation!

As the days passed it became increasingly evident that the theology held by each man in the discussion was not quite the same, and there developed an air of unease in the house.

Before he left Jim asked me to go for a short walk with him. He wanted to talk to me on my own, which would not have been possible in the house.

We walk a short way up the road, he then stood by the gate to the field I knew so well.

I knew almost every blade of grass in that field as I had spent a lot of time in it, doing the morning and evening milking outside in the field in the summer months. This was my familiar ground and one I felt safe in.

As he leaned against the gate he told me it was evident to him that our father loved us very much, but would I consider that there was a possibility that he could be wrong about some things?

It took me a brief moment to realise the enormity of what I had just heard.

I was now 19 years old and nobody had challenged me directly regarding the relationship I had with my father and my father's attitude to his own beliefs.

I had been sheltered from direct confrontation.

I trusted my father, and didn't want to embrace the thought he could be wrong.

I saw at a glance what this idea could lead to.

Life was tough, but the Bible never promised an easy life for a christian while here on earth.

In fact, if life was too easy, it implied that you were compromising your faith somewhere, you were not as pure and untarnished a christian as one should be.

There were many aspects of my father I didn't find easy, but thinking he might be wrong was another dimension altogether.

Also we had come through so much because of his thinking and I couldn't allow those experiences to be so lightly invalidated by such thoughts.

I believed that what I had been taught was the truth, and felt secure in that belief and it wasn't for me to decide if it was right or wrong

But I was being asked to consider.

So consider I would, knowing that to think my father could or maybe wrong in some matters was the unthinkable.

He was our father, our god-given head, the one who had brought us up, and provided the best he could for us, in the best way he knew how.

My father had told me once."always remember, you *could* be wrong", but of course that applied to me. The 'you' meant me not him. I could be wrong.

Whilst the thought that I could be wrong was embraceable and very likely, the thought that he could be wrong was very disturbing and we had had enough disturbances in our lives. I didn't need any more.

However, both these men were as formidable as each other and equally 'right in their own eyes' and sooner or later I could see the inevitable happening.

But actually, the matter which in the end was the tipping point was not theology at all!

Jim gave me the gist of what the controversial matter between him and my father was, and of course it came down to a matter of authority.

My father had told Jim that he didn't want me married until I was 21. Jim had taken that to mean that at 21 I could be married, so therefore as the promise for the future was secure a commitment now would be in order.

My father however, maintained that he said, he would consider the possibility of me being married only when I was 21, and therefore there was only a promise of a possibility.

It was a fine point, but one which neither of them were prepared to concede.

I knew full well, that the more anyone argued with my father, the more they lost his respect, co-operation and communication.

Our father had met his match and they both were like two bulls having a stand-off.

I hated being stuck in the middle even though I desperately wanted to find a way forward out of our situation.

I wasn't the only one wondering if anyone would be good enough for us - if anyone would get our father's approval.

Jim was the fourth person who was having difficulties with our father about us and none of the others worked out as they had initially wanted.

Eventually my father stopped Jim and I writing to each other (until I was 21, the following year) and wanted Jim could show his respect by complying).

Jim found his way round this and started to write to my sister for help in getting through to me, and get a sense of my own thoughts on the matter.

He was pushing for a commitment from me, which he believed was in order with my father's promise.

This put me in a very difficult and unhappy position.

I would be 21 the following year, so why not wait, be respectful to both my father and me and understand that putting pressure on me would only add stress and difficulty.

After weeks of pushing me into believing him and eventually giving me an ultimatum that I would commit to him now or he would walk away, I gave Jim through my sister, a commitment.

It was not how I had imagined things would be.

A girl has dreams of such a day!

This was anything but a fulfilment of those dreams.

Jim arrived unexpectedly on the doorstep a few weeks later.

He stood on the doorstep, probably expecting to be invited in, but he wasn't invited in at all. He was told to return the following day.

He did arrive the next day as agreed, taking pride in being a man of his word.

He spoke with my father for a long time and after they concluded whatever they needed of say to each other, my father told me to get ready to go for a walk with him.

I had never known my father to take a walk, ever. This was most unusual.

We put our coats on and set off, with him leading the way, finally reaching the moor I knew so well from the winter days of catching rabbits, the summer days from gathering mushrooms, and the days in-between from gathering firewood.

Today I was experiencing a side of my father I seldom saw and which made me worried as it was so unusual, though I had seen small glimpses of it in the distant past. He was showing what seemed a more approachable, fatherly and caring side. His manner was kind and somewhat more gentle than normal and he used his softer tone of voice.

He chose a spot sheltered among the gorse bushes to sit down. Making himself as comfortable as he could, and with me sitting down at his side, he started to talk.

He laid out in precise detail the way that a god-honouring engagement and marriage takes place.

He went into minute detail of moral obligations, god-given headship, a woman's duty, a mother's duty, sibling duty, submission, biblical principles, ownership of headship.

An hour later he was still talking.

Two hours later the explanations went on.

Three hours he kept going on.

I had little to say, he wanted me to listen, so I listened as long as he kept talking.

Four hours he was still going.

Every minuscule, infinitesimal, microscopic detail of how things 'should' be done was gone over.

Five hours later he was still in full swing.

Did I understand?

Yes, all had been fully explained.

Six hours still he was talking.

Then seven hours.

Non-stop I had listened to what God wants in a good moral order of the family.

As the sun went down, he decided it was time we returned home.

I was exhausted and my head was spinning.

My ears were ringing:

'God'.

'Moral'

'Obey'.

'Right'.

'Right way'.

'Obey and bless'.

In all of the explanations going on in his head, he repeated many things.

He repeated what he had told us years before, that if a young christian girl wanted to get married, she just had to tell her father, he would take up the matter and start finding someone for her, or she could suggest someone to him (or 'them' if both her parents were there) - after consideration was made by her family, she would have the final say, that is if the family said yes, she could decide no, but if the family said no, then no it was.

Perhaps he had forgotten that I had actually followed to the letter that very pattern which he was now propounding, and he had conveniently forgotten his response to my approach to him, which was certainly very different to what he was now portraying to be the god-honouring way.

When I had approached him in the manner now instructed by him, about a year before – my whole being was promptly dismissed with a huff and I was curtly reminded of my age.

We arrived home to find it was now 8.00pm and the supper was well over-cooked, but the family had waited for us to join them before starting.

To my surprise, Jim was at the supper table.

We ate in silence all eyes downcast. I had lost my appetite and wanted nothing.

We were all told to stay seated as my father rose and left the room.

There was a seriousness and authority in his voice which implied "don't mess with me."

He returned with his Bible and to his place at the head of the table.

Like a judge opening a legal document giving him authority, he opened his bible to the book of Numbers.

He read the whole of chapter 30 with great solemnity.

He repeated:

"If a woman also vow a vow unto the Lord, and bind herself by a bond, being in her father's house in her youth; and her father hear her vow, and her bond wherewith she has bound her soul, and her father shall hold his peace at her: then all her vows shall stand - - - but if her father disallow her in the day that he heareth; not any of her vows, or of her bonds, wherewith she hath bound her soul, shall stand, and the Lord shall forgive her, because her father disallowed her." verses 3-5.

He declared that he was disallowing any agreement I had made with Jim from that moment. He had heard of our agreement the evening before, and as the Jewish day started at sundown he was within the time-frame of "In the day that he heareth" within the 24 hours of hearing of it.

My mind was a quagmire of unclear thoughts all jumbled up, my nerves singing like a harp, making my thoughts go into a mass of flying atoms whizzing around in space, with nowhere to go.

All I wanted was peace and unity not this Judaism of authority to get one's own way.

I heard Jim say to me "do you agree with your father?"

"How could he?"

"How could he put me in this position!"

"Make me choose between him and my father – disrupt a family, divide a family?"

I was tired, very tired of conflict and I heard a small voice say "Yes."

It was my voice.

Jim rose from the table and walked out of the house.

I could see all prospects walking out with him and I wanted to shout out after him to come back and see things from my point of view.

Just a little patience and all would have worked out well.

There had been no need for all this debacle.

But he was gone and left a heavy silence in our kitchen as each of us tried to assimilate what had just happened in a kitchen, in Scotland, in 1981.

As the silence set in I experienced a deep sense of shame.

I had caused such stress in the family.

I was the cause extreme measures were used.

Although my father had told me what was right and I had in the end complied with him, the sense of shame wasn't eased.

I went to bed and stayed there for two weeks.

The weather was breaking into winter and so were my feelings.

The daylight was short and the darkness long, reflecting the state I was in.

Unable to get up as usual in the morning, I hid under the covers as I reflected on the guilt and shame I so keenly felt.

My father's attitude towards me didn't change much to my surprise. I expected he would increase his displeasure, but nothing was added to the usual frowns.

He was such an enigma.

For the first time I felt separated emotionally from my sisters, which was of my own doing, the result of my actions, and this increased into a very deep sense of loneliness.

I sank into a place of deep despondency doubting a good future and with the prospect of remaining exactly where I was for as long as I was alive.

Any hope in prayers changing things had a tough time.

Thankfully I had the goats, the only thing which kept me going, kept life moving on.

They needed feeding, milking and cleaning.

Esther especially was a great comfort as I poured out my emotions to her and she just listened and responded unconditionally.

I started to look at my father actions separately from his teachings.

He had just used the Bible in a way which he had never done before.

His argument against the order of the Amish, was that they took the Old Testament too literally –

What had he just done?

He had taken Numbers chapter 20 and applied it in the most literal way possible.

Whilst I could understand how the 'disallowing' concept fitted into his thinking on the role of woman, I couldn't fathom his use of the Jewish day beginning at sundown.

The belief that the New Testament superseded the Old Testament was a fundamental part of the Christian faith which he held.

So why had he gone back into the Old Testament?

For any other reason that it suited his purpose?

My personal faith was tried as I began to absorb a lot of guilt. I knew that it wasn't the holy, righteous people that God accepted, but those who knew and acknowledged their need of him and I certainly did that every day, God's love and mercy however, seemed far from me at this time.

I went to the dark place where guilt thrives, and though there was life in my soul, there was a very cold world outside of it.

The October gales thrashed against the windows in sympathy with my inner turmoil and disquiet.

# Chapter Nineteen

Slowly I started to be able to feel as though I could breathe again and that life had to go on.

Our outward misery continued as money was now incredible short most of the time and sometimes there simply wasn't any.

We had to start to find different ways each of us could earn a little money with our limiting circumstances. No reliable transport, or electricity supply, no phone, no computer or typewriter. Just ourselves and the handcraft skills we had.

I used the knitting machine given to us by our aunt to make uniform jerseys for the local school. We were also hand-knitting for a local craft shop being paid for each ball we knitted. It was all a pittance but every penny counted. There were days when we would desperately try and finish a garment, cycle the six miles to the craft shop, and get eggs for supper with the money just received, forming a perfect self-perpetuating circle of existence.

I received an order to make an adults jumper which I duly made and waited to be paid for it. The only way I could be paid was by cash or Postal Order. I was eager to get paid and decided that I would let my father know that I was still waiting for the money. He told me that I had been paid for my work! I was surprised and waited for him to explain.

"You belong to me and everything you own therefore belongs to me". That therefore included the payment for any work I did. A Cheque had been sent made payable to him as I didn't have a bank account. He quite happily took whatever he wanted. Of course, I realised that I was working to in order to provided for the food I was eating, but it would have been nice to have had the opportunity of handling the money I earned and respectfully given it to him, rather than he take ownership without so much as a blink of acknowledgement of where it had come from. Surely he should have known that it was counter-productive to just take earnings, and that I would have been far more motivated to work if I had seen the fruits of my labour.

The evening readings continued, but more were added on a Sunday afternoon and were done in the sitting room. We were not attending church regularly at this time, and our father started a 'service' of some sort in the house. We would sing a few Psalms and then listen to Parliamentary Sermons (1640-50) which were exceeding long, very academic and intricate.

The chairs in the sitting room had long since worn out, the webbing holding the cushion one sat on, was broken in every chair, and we had put planks of woods or cardboard under the cushion to stop ourselves falling through. They were large chairs which were far too big for my small frame and were intensely uncomfortable.

And it was so very cold. Too cold to concentrate properly, and too cold to fall asleep. Sometimes we would hide a hot water bottle behind our backs to make the time more bearable. Our father would stand at the end of the blanket chest for the whole time - reading, prayers and singing – so what had we to complain about, we were sitting!

I don't expect mine was the only mind that wondered the earth during these long sessions.

Some months later, our father gave permission for me to visit my sister who had been sent to look after our brother who was going through a difficult time.

We talked in the kitchen about how she was settling in and what she was doing and to my utter amazement Jim walked in.

They had maintained contact with each other as best they could and now where very obviously close friends as least.

True to his style Jim was still oblivious to his surroundings talking about a point of theology how God has decided before our birth what happens in this life. Everything that happens is planned by God.

No wonder he went on about God foreordaining everything, they decided to tell me they were engaged!

God had foreordained them to be together, not me and that's why things had ended for me the way they did.

So, God's purpose will be worked out.

Interesting!

Life does go on and I had to go on with it, though there were times when I really didn't want to. I would have much preferred to have entered a black hole and not come back out of it.

I was in an emotional vacuum.

I felt nothing but darkness, shame and guilt.

Everything was cold, very cold. The house was cold, the weather was cold and the family around me were also cold.

The future looked cold, uninspiring, dark and hopeless.

Life was ebbing away in emotional hypothermia.

I desperately needed a sense of warmth to feel life again.

I was graving warmth like one starved of food.

I didn't feel forgiven or trusted by those in whose care I was, but I understood and carried the guilt of it, and believed it was no more than I deserved.

The warmth, support and love received from the chapel in Wales when I was ten was long lived out and now a distant memory.

I was the one who had let expectations down and the coldness and suspicion I was treated with, reminded me of that every waking moment.

We had lived for, and devoted our life to the ideal and I had broken that mold.

The mold of holiness, godliness, virtue and above all trust.

Months of desolateness and loneliness passed and the long winter became spring, but nothing changed with the season, and I trudged every day up and the road tending to the goats who were about to kid.

# Chapter Twenty

There was a knock on the door and I opened it with caution to find on the doorstep neighbour who was known to our family.

Not connected to the church he was nevertheless someone I thought I could trust and who, more importantly I believed my father trusted.

He had come to ask if we could help him as he had been put out of his house by his wife and had to move into a caravan. Immediately he needed help with his clothes' washing until he sorted things out.

He offered to pay us, and his offer of payment was too good for my father to refuse given we were so very short of money and necessities.

I was given the job of washing his bags of clothes, the amount which I could hardly believe one person could possibly wear in only a few days.

We were used to making our one change of outer clothes last for weeks!

I hand washed all his muddy, filthy sweaty clothes.

He would sometimes come and pick up the bag of clean laundry or I would cycle to his caravan, hand them over and receive the welcome payment.

On an occasion he came to the house when I was by myself, my father and sister having taken a trip into town.

Before long he had taken complete advantage of me and told me that I had to continue satisfying him or he would tell my father what had happened.

I knew he had put a noose around my neck and if I pulled it, I would hang myself.

I was determined not to hang myself for as long as I possibly could.

I wouldn't hang myself of course, but my father might (figuratively) and I would do anything and everything I possible could to ensure that didn't happen.

I knew of my fathers' believe in his own authority and the way he used it with his family, and that he was quite capable of changing my life forever if he wanted to.

Every day I was told by Charlie when to go to him, and it didn't matter when in the twenty-four hour clock that would be. I got the summons and the threat, and had to obey day or night.

He would leave a letter under a stone on the grass verge outside the house. I was told that I had to reply to his letters and leave the reply under the same stone.

Many were the times he wanted me to go to his place in the night and I would crawl out of bed, into the darkness and the icy cold, put on a few warm jumpers and tights and creep down the stairs making sure they didn't creak enough to wake anyone, pass through the old squeaky door, close it behind me and secure it, make my way through the old disused part of the house, through the back door and out to brave the elements.

The mile walk was often eerily quiet and I learned much about night life as I made my way past long empty stretches of wasteland and hearing the grasses rustling in the night air.

In the height of summer it barely got dark, and those were the more frightening nights, as strange shadows fluttered and hovered over the countryside and bounced around me in all directions as though someone was laughing at me and playing games with my mind. The complete blackness and cold of the winter was far more preferable than watching the haunting summer shadows dance around.

Every shadow had a heavy weight attached to it, overstimulating my already frayed nerves.

Many times during those night walks I cast my mind back to my bed and it's warmth and hanker after its comfort and peace and wondering when and how this nightmare would end.

Those thoughts only reinforced my determination to make my own way out of this, but eventually I started to feel I was in too deep and the whole matter was too big for me.

There were times when I felt overwhelmed and oppressed beyond measure with guilt, and had the sense of being 'crushed down' with a burden which would break me if I carried it much longer or if it got any heavier.

I longed for someone to share my burden with, to have advice from, to listen to me without judgement – but there was no-one.

Relentlessly he made his demands of me, and I had couldn't find a solution.

Every possible chance he put the pressure on and I would have to find a way to conform.

There might have been a way out, but I couldn't see it.

He had threatened me so often that he would tell my father and he didn't threaten just once, it was a repeated threat, and one which I didn't know if it would be only words. Although I realised that he was using my fear to force conformity, I didn't know him well enough to know if he was capable of carrying those threats out.

But I did experience he was capable of hurting me.

One day after calling me to the barn in the field where I grazed my goats, I found his hand against my throat as he pinned me to wall. He did hurt, and so I had reason to wonder if he would indeed take revenge if I stood up to him.

Time and again I thought about how to outmanoeuvre him, to outsmart him, but I couldn't think of a way.

Getting through every day took all my energy and strength, and even in the night I had no respite.

In the morning the cycle would start all over again.

My strength was slowly but surely waning.

But I simply couldn't contemplate my father finding out.

The idea of my family finding out was the very worst of all options.

Nothing could shake my fear of what might happen to me if I didn't comply.

I held onto the strong conviction, the certain knowledge that "my father would imprison me if he found out".

I feared for my future, and this blinding fear was very real. I was convinced that my fear was not just a reaction but a rational fear, and that what I was fearing could indeed become a reality.

I expressed my deepest fear to Charlie in the words "if you tell my father, he will imprison me". I believed this to be the actual, the real, the certain outcome of my father finding out what had happened, but I didn't realise that sharing this very real fear, it would be used as a weapon and threat against me.

I had revealed my achilles tendon, he pulled his arrow and hit bullseye.

He now had me in his hand like a puppy.

"Yes sir, yes sir, whatever you say sir".

Some of what was going through my emotions was the sheer guilt of being taken advantage of.

"If only I had - - -"

"Been stronger and resisted"

"If only I had - - -"

"If only"

"It's my fault"

I had learned over years to absorb blame at all times and in all situations.

I was nothing, accounted for nothing and meant nothing.

What should have been a sacred moment in my life had been completely violated. I was now defiled, dirty, unholy, unclean and this was added to all the guilt I was already carrying from earlier. I felt as though I was a 'marked' person.

Once the shock and my emotions had calmed a little, I settled with the only thing I could think of: the Old Testament declaration of a wife needing to produce a 'token of virginity' to her husband and to her father, to prove her purity.

I could not now produce this, which would mean that I could no longer be considered for a wife, which was the only 'biblically right' destiny of a woman.

I would be disgraced for ever, as long as I lived.

In the forefront of my mind was the Old Testament directive about a woman's virtue and what should happen to her if she didn't have it.

I remembered how my father had taken another Old Testament passage and applied it to our present life, and knew he wouldn't hesitate to use the same principle if he had wanted to – it would only be logical for him to do so and I was full of trepidation, fear and tears.

I thought of my life now as a life that was finished, a mere existence.

I was completely nothing, not even worthless.

I was now in a situation where I was given a stark choice, doing something which I thoroughly hated and knew was wrong, or risk my father finding out and being at the mercy of his reactions.

It didn't need thinking about.

Instinctively I chose to take my future into my own hands and see if I could possibly find a way out by myself and 'save my own skin'.

If I could do this, then I might just possibly survive into something more than the proverbial 'old bitter spinster' with a reputation attached, locked into a house and kept away from society as the shame of the family.

But I had very little to fight with.

I had no self-respect left at all and no mental strength.

Mental strength was important as conviction can produce strength and I had none.

I hadn't long before this, in one of my more courageous teenage moments of quiet theoretical debates with my father, posed the question, about what a woman in submission should do, if her head tells her to do something which is wrong.

"Does her loyalty lie directly with God?" And could there be an occasion in life which could allow her to overrule her headship?

The answer – Her responsibility is to obey her God-given moral headship, and what he directs her to do is his responsibility before God.

I could see that this thought negated all responsibility from women.

I had my own thoughts about this answer, but didn't want to take it further with him as he had the remarkable ability to talk me out of my instinctive thought and make sure I ended up agreeing with him whatever.

Besides women don't think, they obey!

Obedience was being drummed into me no matter what was developing within me as a thinking teenager wanting to broaden my horizons into womanhood.

Unfortunately I did have a brain – and couldn't help using it.

My brain worked whether I wanted it to or not.

Thoughts kept coming no matter how hard I tried to quieten them.

The 'what if's", the 'but's' of a young mind, all quashed and answered with some biblical principle or quotation.

One afternoon ihad been called to my father's room and I stood by the door as he silently paced his room.

The atmosphere was tense and I had no idea why I had been called to see him.

I then realised that his bedroom window overlooked a small moorland piece where I had recently had to meet up with Charlie.

I started to feel light-headed I was so nervous.

I thought the ultimate had happened – he had seen us, and I was standing before him now as a criminal stands before a judge about to be handed their sentence.

"What were you doing on the moor?" he asked in a quiet voice.

Fuzz, fuzz, fuzz was all I could hear after that.

Thoughts went flying in and out.

"you've never bothered with us before – sleeping in till the afternoon."

"You never watched over us as we grew up or showed any care how we spent the day"

"Why now?"

"What did you see?"

"What - - - fuzz, fuzz, then quietly fading fuuuzzzz

His figure pacing the room in silence become blurred and then -
I was on the floor.

Coming round slowly I was handed a cup of tea.

After drinking the tea I was sent to my room.

This fainting episode highlighted to me just how on the edge I was living and how stressed I was.

The situation was getting too much and I was becoming a nervous wreck.

For two years I had endured the situation, the disturbed nights, the midnight walks, the fear of being found out, and above all, the fear of what it was doing to my own faith, confidence and conscience.

Adrenaline had become my survival medicine.

Now I was beginning to think that I simply couldn't go on as things were.

I realised as my strength and health were declining, that I might in the end be better off at the mercy of my family, take whatever was my due, than continue to carry my burden on my own.

I could hardly believe I was contemplating telling my father what I had spent two years trying to hide.

I had been driven to despair in the choices before me and the choice I had made was fast becoming impossible to live up to.

I hadn't found a way out.

I hadn't resolved it by myself.

Nothing I said or did had made any difference to the demands Charlie continued to put on me and I was constantly reminded what would happen if I didn't continue to answer the demands.

After much thought I made a decision.

I wrote about what I was going through, about my situation, explaining down my difficulties, including my dilemma about everything.

I put the paper I had written it all down on, under my pillow for the night wanting to find a way to send it by post to our mother.

Mother – what a concept!

But I had no envelope and no stamp.

Our mother had recently sent us an Easter card forwarding us her new address.

If ever a girl needed her mother it was now.

I went to bed wondering how I was going to get this letter to the post.

For the first time in my life, I felt the luxury of having two parents.

If one didn't understand me, maybe the other one would.

Yes, it was a luxury and one which I needed to call in now.

I woke as my father entered my bedroom.
I sensed I hadn't been asleep for long.
It was still dark and I knew my father was a night owl and didn't do things in the morning.

He told me to get up and indicated with a sideways thrust of his head that I should follow him to his room.

Of course I obeyed, silently like a lamb to the slaughter, I was led to the 'inner room' which I could tonight have so easily have called the 'slaughter house'.

He closed his bedroom door behind us and started to pace the floor relentlessly with an agitated silence.

I was determined not to faint again.
I waited for him to speak.
I waited.
The tension grew.
He kept pacing.

I continued to wait for what seemed like ages, and I worked hard at making sure my nerves would be as strong as they needed to be for whatever was happening now.

I wondered if he would ever find words.
He was a man of few words, but never of no words.
Finally he managed to fumble out something about what was going on in my life and his focus was on
"Why?"
He repeated over and over.
"Why?"
"Why didn't you tell me?"
I was only just managing to hold myself together.

How on earth was I going to explain any of this situation to him in a way he could possibly understand?

I saw a piece of paper in his hand.
I recognised the paper as the letter I had written to my mother which I had put under my pillow.
I was dumbstruck.
Fuzz, fuzz.

"No, no fuzzing allowed right now. Stand your ground and be strong" I heard myself say to someone listening inside of me.

I realised that my sister must have searched my bed, found the letter and given it him and now I was facing his reaction full in the face.

The reaction I had so dreaded for the past two years and did everything I could to avoid.

Now my future was very clearly in his hands.

He would deal with it in his own way.

Looking straight at me he asked again "Why?"

"Because I was frightened." I replied demurely.

"Why?"

"Because our relationship isn't what it should be".

"Oh, you thing that do you? And what do you think it should be?"

"I just think I shouldn't be afraid of you".

His face turned into an expression which I expected – dismissive, belittling, disbelieving, scornful.

Finally the long dreaded scenario had happened in front of me, but I knew he wasn't finished dealing with me yet.

I was sent back to bed, and spent the rest of the night wondering what would be his next move.

If he did not 'imprison' me I would be very surprised, but how that 'imprisonment' would actually look like in reality I didn't know and couldn't think about, but I believed I knew him well enough to know what sort of future was about to be mine.

Tossing and turning in bed, I kept hearing unusual noises all night.

There was strange banging, like a hammering sound, and my father footsteps walking up and down the stairs albeit quietly.

I didn't want to know what he was doing, so I pulled the blankets over my head.

I didn't want the daylight to come with the revelations it would bring, and I certainly didn't want to face my sister who was unswervingly loyal to our father.

Daylight broke and morning followed, and to my dismay my father was up and about, having worked throughout the night securing all the net curtains and windows closed. He explained to me in rather a subdued tone that "It's not that I want to keep you in, it's to keep others out".

"No difference" I thought.

My sister was given a key to the front door, and I could only go out chaperoned by her at all times, including going into the garden to empty to kitchen waste.

The back door was kept locked at all times.

So -

Yes, my fears had indeed been very real, and whatever was claimed, I was to all intents 'imprisoned'.

I could roam around the house under the watchful eye of my sister.

That was my life now and for the foreseeable future.

I tried to resign myself to it, to this state of disgraced hibernation.

My faith took me into a dark place of carrying a burden of guilt and shame and I was struggling.

Like a dry sponge I soaked up all the guilt I could possibly absorb and was extremely sensitive to the acerbic attitude shown toward me at home.

Tensions in the house were high.

My father was quiet and displayed an aura of stiffness.

He seemed stressed and distant more than normal for him.

He hung around the kitchen a lot more than normal.

I felt as though he had waited for things to go 'wrong' before he showed any interest in our daily life, having spent years reading through the night and rising well into the day and then making us leave the kitchen and go elsewhere when he was up and having 'breakfast'.

He was lucky that we were so obedient, conscientious and compliant.

I was so worried what future I was now assigned to, and whether he would use the Old Testament directive of punishment against me, which would mean that I would be under his governance till his death and that I would be so in a state of disgrace, that I had to ask him to discuss the passage which worried me so much (Deuteronomy 22) and his understanding of its application in my life. He assured me that I had nothing to fear regarding not being a virgin. He would not consider the matter of relevance regarding a future marriage.

I didn't need to understand the nuances of his thinking, I was just very relieved.

However, if I wasn't going to be punished, then he must have believed that I wasn't completely responsible' and if he thought that, then why didn't he make more effort to remove the ongoing attitude which made me feel over-burdened with guilt.

But perhaps my logic and his were different, or maybe he just didn't understand emotional needs, or it just didn't fit his purpose to use this passage like he had used the other one years before.

For now I was just relieved and given a slither of hope, even living behind the securely closed windows, doors and curtains that maybe, just maybe this would not be my life forever and that this place would not be my home forever.

# Chapter Twenty-One

Sitting at the kitchen table while I stood by the door, our father told me to "come here" and indicated with his finger towards his feet.

I didn't react.

His tone was harsh and sharp.

I did nothing but stay fixed to the floor.

I was completely mentally and physically exhausted but found the strength from somewhere to make a very precise decision that I wasn't going to be spoken to as if I was a dog.

I had had more than enough and something living very deeply inside of me rose to the surface.

I knew that I couldn't go lower than I already was and still survive.

In spite of knowing that I had been told to do something and that obedience was the acceptable response, no obedience was forthcoming.

My feet were still fixed firmly to the floor and my legs refused to move.

I stood by the door refusing obedience and feeling nothing but icy cold inside.

I for once stood up for myself and replied,

"No, I'm not a dog".

I could hardly believe I had outrightly said 'no' to my father.

The worm had turned and looked him full in the face.

I was told go upstairs to my room.

I stayed there in my room for a short while with an inner cold, numbness, and feeling completely emotionless and resigned to whatever was to be, before my father came in with a stick in his hand.

In fact it was a piece of dado rail.

He told me that I had no right to answer him back and that he was going to punish me for being disobedient.

I knew what was coming.

Like my brother all those years ago facing punishment in the name of christian duty, only now I was 22 years old not 14, a young woman and not a boy.

How many stripes would I be getting?

I wouldn't survive 22 – I knew that much.

Thankfully there was no-one else watching - I was spared that humiliation at least.

He told me to bend over.

I was grateful to be wearing a thick woollen tweed skirt with box pleats in it giving me extra layers of thickness.

I bent over the end of the spare bed which had been my sisters, and I waited.

Strike one.

It reverberated across and up into my back.

Strike two.

Humiliation.

Strike three.

Intrinsically broken.

Being on the receiving end, one never sees the rod coming down, and so one doesn't know the moment it's going to land and send shivers right through you and it becomes a matter of bracing oneself in anticipation of the pain.

Not being able to see my father's face giving me the rod, meant I couldn't see what I had hoped for – that it was as painful for him to give it, as it was for me to receive.

He left without a word and I crawled slowly under the bed feeling the need of solid cover and protection.

It was an instinctive move which needed no thought process.

Before this, I'd thought I couldn't possibly feel any lower, but this was another depth altogether. A depth I had no understanding of.

Going under the cover of the bed was in keeping with my emotions.

It was the right and only place for me to be.

Here I had something to cover me, to protect me and being curled up in a ball, in the foetal position gave a feeling of emotional sympathy, protection and strength which I so much needed.

I wasn't long under the bed when my father came in and told me to get out.

This was very hard and was something everything in me screamed not to do.

I just needed time to process what had happened and my reactions to it and felt that he only added to the violence by not giving me that time, but obedience was being drummed into me no matter what.

He didn't call me out for anything particular. Nothing was happening in the house, so I was left thinking he just didn't want me under the bed nursing my hurts.

I was no longer able to pick up letters from Charlie, or leave any letters to be picked up and he had no idea what had happened, so he called the police to our house, making the report that someone was being kept against their will.

The police officers wanted to speak with everyone in the house and I was called into the sitting room last of all.

I couldn't sit down on the chair to talk to the officers without wincing in pain.

I couldn't see scars from the beating, but I could most certainly feel them.

Every time I moved, I was reminded of the emotional state I was in, of the pain, disgrace and the humiliation.

How was I going to get through, heal and come out the other side?

But I could only concentrate on the present. The future was another day to be faced when it came.

I sat there in discomfort answering a few questions from the officers.

This situation all seemed so futile, so irrelevant, so ineffective.

The trouble was, the questioning of the police was all in the presence of my sister.

Anything I would say would be reported back – to the person who had made it impossible to sit without pain - just like my letter was, and what the consequences of that might be I couldn't possibly contemplate.

Having no idea how the 'system' worked, or what support might be available and fearing that speaking out might just cause further pain at home, I had no option but to keep quiet.

If only - -.

The officers left with nothing and no idea of what they had just walked into.

They heard what they needed to and no action was required.

My father and sister were now definitely in charge of everything and I dared not cause any more problems

A few hours later, I was in the car with my father being taken somewhere.

After several hours of travelling, we arrived at the home of a Christian family we had known for a couple of years, where I was left to stay for "a break".

It struck me that my father had the knack of dismissing me when problems arose.

The action he took now reminded me of the "banishment" to England a few years previously.

I felt this very keenly indeed. This was a time when I needed above all things reassurance of his love. I wanted him to take me in his arms and give me a fatherly hug, imparting the message of my inclusion into his affections and thoughts, but instead if this he chose to send me away.

Send me away, and with me all the associated trouble, challenges and disturbances, so he could continue getting up late, drink endless cups of coffee, read books and enjoy my sister's company.

These things didn't go unnoticed and I desperately wanted to be angry, but 'christian' woman don't get angry, so it festered into a deep resentment and then hurt which developed into further estrangement from him in my heart.

Of all the things he did, I found this one of the hardest things to cope with.

I had no idea if the family I was left to stay with had any idea of why I was there at such short notice. I worried endlessly about it. Worried about what their reactions were if they did know. I worried about being judged on the quiet. Being whispered about in my absence. I worried about everything – the "what if's" the "what not's" and any imaginary "but's"

I asked one of the girls, what they knew about my visit and I was reassured that all they knew was I needed "a break".

Of course I was relieved, but as this family were quite strict I was still worried about the "What if's" - if they did know the truth. I felt a bit hypocritical being there without the full extent of the family dynamics known.

Oh so naive!

I really wanted to keep to myself during my stay. I wasn't confident in anything, in any situation, in myself or in anyone else.

I wanted to be reclusive.

I was also suffering from a severe bout of cystitis and all the inconvenience that came with it. Needless to say, I was not getting any treatment for it and neither did anyone know about it.

This family worshipped on their own, in their own setting of a family church, the 'minister' living separately in the attic of the house.

On the two Sundays which I was there, I sat with them and listened to more preaching, but my mind was almost as far from the subject preached as it could be. I needed time to process things, and didn't need more theology to help.

Maybe that's what my father was getting in sending me away – space and peace to deal with things in his own mind.

The 'minister' in this home church was Peter, and one of his jobs was to do the washing-up after lunch every day.

I was asked to dry the dishes.

Of course I would oblige being asked to help as guest in the home, but I didn't really have a heart to do this, as it meant talking to Peter, who seemed quite eager to break up the monotony of his day with chatting.

I must have put a good front on.

A few days before I left Peter invited me to join him for his daily constitutional along the promenade.

With nothing other to do, I agreed and we got windswept in the rough east sea breeze. It felt so good and therapeutic to be once again, outside in the fresh air and actually enjoying company, something I been unable to do for a long time.

I managed to put aside my anxiety for that short afternoon, greatly benefiting by the more 'normal' experience of the simple things in life.

Life had become so complicated with rules and regulations. The suffocating and intrusive 'thou shalt's' and 'thou shalt not's' sucked one's life out, mine anyway.

On my return home I was very surprised to find a letter from Peter and hoped it wasn't what I thought it might be.

How would I cope if it was?

What was it that others could possibly see in me, which I certainly didn't and which I'm quite sure my family didn't either?

He had written to my father to ask permission to write to me.

Not again!

What could go wrong this time!

Everything!

In keeping with his character Peter was always gentle but direct.

My father raised no objections and I received many sweet letters from someone who seemed to really understand me at last. He wrote a poem about the "girl who understood the true meaning of tears" – yes, he had the measure of me and for that I was grateful.

My father noticed I had become a better person since Peter and I became friends, and encouraged our correspondence.

Our tutor also saw good potential stating "It's essential, absolutely essential that you marry an older man. You need a substitute father". She did however, say that I should not do anything without my father's approval as that would not make me happy.

I was so surprised at her comment as she never, ever said anything other than what was supportive about our father. Now, for the first time she showed concern and had an opinion.

Our letters were frequent, and Peter decided to come up to visit.

I was glad, but couldn't help worrying about how he and my father would get on knowing that there was a least one very fundamental difference in their theology.

His visit was very pleasant and I thoroughly appreciated his sense of humour and we got on very well, despite the age difference of twenty years.

Of course theology had to come into the equation and it became a stumbling block. My father decided that Peter needed to agree on one particular point of doctrine, knowing it was the very thing Peter had made a stand about in his ministry.

As expected Peter didn't think it was as important for him and my father to agree, as it was for him and me to agree. It was, after all me he was contemplating living with not my father, and so he wanted to by-pass my father in the matter which he knew they would never agree on.

My father took this as an affront to his authority and started to 'return to sender' Peter's letters to me.

It hurt me knowing that Peter would think it was me returning them.

He couldn't have known that there was no way I would have responded like that at all.

Unfortunately Peter believed that it was me, and so the matter ended on a sour note with pleasant memories.

The frustration of being the sandwich filling in the middle of two intractable people and of not being understood or taken into account really got to me one day, and in reaction to that frustration I threw my bible as hard as I could onto the floor saying to myself that I wanted nothing to do with christianity if this is what it was like.

I was sorry to see that I had damaged the spin of my bible and realised that I had a momentary and emotional reaction, which was rather short-lived.

# Chapter Twenty-Two

Our local church had a communion service scheduled for Sunday.

On Saturday evening we attended the preparatory service and after the service the minister took me aside quietly and said that the church were not happy about me taking part in the communion in the light of what had happened with Charlie, and until they were satisfied that I had repented and been remorseful I was being asked to absent myself.

What did they think 'had happened?'

I naturally absorbed more guilt and shame, this time added by the 'church'.

This church included John.

This sort of disgrace never happened in 'the church' and they were unprepared to deal with it.

Needing to comply with their wish caused me great distress.

"If the church couldn't accept me – would Christ?"

"Did forgiveness depend on repentance?"

"What exactly did I need to repent of?"

"How would they know if I had 'repented' and repented in such a way which would satisfy them?"

"How could they possibly judge my inner being?"

They had simply passed judgement on me without asking one single question.

Dejected and rejected I had only myself to try and make some sense of the situation.

Theology was of no help at this point.

All the theology in the world couldn't make up for the need I had of my family's love.

I started to doubt in the love of God. I believed that I had every reason to think God's love was removed, and it had been removed a long distance from me, by those who professed to be his people.

Many days of spiritual doubt and fear were spent as I increasingly battled with the knowledge that God's love covers all, but not what I now was or had become and certainly not how I was feeling.

Sitting by myself in the kitchen one night too disturbed and haunted to take rest I battled with the balance of sin and forgiveness, with the heavy burden of guilt, and with the feeling that I had become unforgivable.

In my contemplations and distress, I was gently surrounded by a remarkable and inexplicable warm blanket which was put over my shoulders and breathed life back into my soul.

Maybe this was God meeting me in my darkest hour.

I knew from then that God would not forsake me, that I had an assurance of his love.

I was able to go to bed, get a restful sleep and start climbing out of the pit of despair I had fallen into.

I realised that the elders and minister must have known something of what had happened but what exactly I had no idea. I was left in the dark and left to my own surmising.

I didn't want to go to church and meet these people again.

It was excruciatingly embarrassing for me to go the services, shake hands at the exit, smile politely - all as if nothing had happened.

I couldn't bear it.

I didn't go for a while, and was very dismayed that no-one from the church enquired about my absence.

I asked my father many times "Why doesn't the minister come to see me?"

"Why doesn't he wonder why I haven't gone to church?"

The minister knew what had happened, and I knew he knew, so couldn't understand why I was just left alone, like nobody cared.

My father's response to my questions was,

"Don't you criticise the minister. You can't open your mouth about anybody".

I asked my father again to make arrangements for me speak to the minister myself.

Eventually he agreed and I spent a few moments with the minister in his study.

There I was told that I had been guilty of the sin of adultery. My whole body went hot and my nerves on edge.

Really?

That was one of the worst of all sins.

The problem was that many of my letters left under the stone had been passed on to the minister by Charlie, and that was the evidence the church had of my sin.

No wonder they didn't ask me anything, obviously presuming that the letters I wrote had been written in full freedom of will.

By now I had no strength left to make an argument for myself, and I was also sure that no-one would believe me anyway.

Anything I could say now, would only look like making feeble excuses.

They had dished out what discipline they wanted, and the matter was now in the past.

The minister assured me that he was satisfied with my repentance and so the issue was no longer of concern.

That may have been true for them, but for me the issue was far from in the past.

My father told me not long after that he had talked the matter over with the minister and that he had decided that he wanted to deal with the matter himself, and that the minister didn't need to see me.

That was the reason I had been left alone.

# Chapter Twenty-Three

Our tutor had now decided it was time for her to return and live with us as she was getting on in age and her health was failing.

She had the room downstairs which was by the front door, and had been used to store her belongings in. In preparation for her arrival the room was tidied up and a bed put in.

The only form of heating in it was a small coal fire, which she lit every day. She bought her own coal which was delivered to the coal room in the back of the house and kept along with our peat bags.

She had been very happy in the Church she was associated with during her time away, which it sounded similar in the way she was looked after by them to what we had experienced with her in Wales many years previously.

Her faith was strong and she spent most of her time in her room reading the Psalms of David and gaining much comfort from them.

As her health slowly got worse and she became weaker she found it difficult to gather and carry fuel for her own fire, but we were told not to help her whenever our father found us doing so.

Our father had the idea that illness was a trial or punishment from God for something not right in one's life.

The notion that one's faith should overcome all, that Christians who walk in the right way, don't get sick was something we got used to.

He had a good/bad, black/white or holy/unholy division in his thinking which had no room for any middle ground.

The reason perhaps that we were not allowed to help our tutor in her life now, was that he believed she needed to take on whatever

God had given her for reasons known only to God. The fact that she had done so much for our family, especially for him in helping with our upbringing, enabling him to pursue his love of reading and living the life of an 'idealist', counted for nothing in her own hour of need.

I was very embarrassed when our neighbours' young son came to the door with kindling for her which he had gathered into a bundle in his small arms.

It seemed as though we couldn't even look after our own, and that other people had a more thoughtful, normal and loving side.

"Was our theology right if it resulted in this kind of attitude to our fellow human beings?" was a question that disturbed me deeply, knowing instinctively that the resounding answer was 'no', something was out of balance.

Unfortunately for her, she was at the receiving end of the 'troubles I had caused' as she was not given a key to the house, so she had to ask for the door to be opened every time she needed to go outside. In effect she was as much a 'prisoner' as I was, through no fault of her own.

She wasn't even allowed to eat with us, and this was something I never liked, wanted, appreciated or understood.

It was now just me and my sister at home and she always cooked main meal which we called supper, and after supper both she and our father would 'retire' up to his bedroom/study and myself and tutor would clear up. I would then spend time on my own until I was invited to go into the 'study' leaving our tutor in her own room, and we would then engage in 'family worship' a custom held by many in Scotland and which we had been doing since our arrival 16 years earlier.

One evening, standing at the kitchen sink doing the dishes our tutor paused briefly and looking down, she said "I'm bleeding".

"Do you need medical help?" I asked her.

"Yes, tell your father I need a nurse."

I went up to our father's room where he and my sister were engaging in their favourite occupation – reading.

I knocked on the door, proceeded to enter, open my mouth in panic and say something along the lines that Judith had asked for medical help and please would you phone for a nurse?

I was promptly told to go back out and re-enter in the correct manner, in order to be heard.

I couldn't do anything right could I?

The contrast was evident. My sister was sitting in front of my father rather like a Victorian Lady of leisure doing the most important things in life – submitting to him, and to God and reading, whilst I was not sophisticated and rushed in with unladylike panic and urgency dealing with real life.

I was disheartened at his response – almost as though he didn't care about the real world and life, unless it was all wrapped in some kind of demure, controlled manner like wrapping paper, which would reach his high standards of behaviour, and didn't care for the kernel of the matter.

I went back out of the door, re-entered his room and made sure I copied the demeanour of a 'Lady of leisure' who had all the time in world to deliver the most useless piece of information possible, with all the correct 'will's, please's, may's' as I could possible add to the pressing issue of medical help required – now.

After ascertaining that the bleeding didn't come from any innocuous part, he agreed to go to the phone, which meant getting up, putting his coat on, getting into his car and driving a mile to the nearest phone box and of course drive back again, retake his position in his chair and pick up his book.

The district nurse responded and after several weeks of being in pain, needing medication and bleeding, our tutor was admitted to hospital and we were informed of her passing a few weeks later.

Her passing left a bit hole in our life. Even though we had learnt to manage in her absences through the years, she had been the one constant in our lives and the one who we would often turn to, sometimes for advice or knowledge, sometimes for encouragement, or sometimes simply for company.

The day of her funeral was very hard, and made so much harder than it needed to be.

Our father had befriended some visitors to the church and invited them over for coffee in the morning. The four of them arrived and were treated as VIP's in the kitchen sharing theology and their understanding of 'ungodliness in Christendom'.

Our father seemed totally oblivious to the time and occasion and talked on and on with these guests, while we were getting very anxious in the sitting room finding the whole thing absurd and inappropriate.

With some 'heat under the collar' he was disturbed by one of us and reminded of the time and occasion – that it was time we paid our respects and laid our beloved friend to her rest.

The guests were very apologetic, not having been told of our family circumstances and left with no further ado.

The emotional coldness he displayed that day was something which disturbed me very much and something I found profoundly disrespectful, especially to the one person who had stood by him and supported him in every way for the past three decades.

He had behaved as though he had no regard for a person, a life, and that theology, principles and theories were what really mattered in life – the rest was of no consequence, significance or relevance.

Our father was doing all he could to stop the impending planned marriage between Jim and my sister.

He was adamant that it wouldn't develop into anything concrete, long-lasting or legal. He put pressure on her by constantly writing letters to her and to anyone who he thought she might listen to, or to anyone who might be in a position of exerting any kind of influence regarding her relationship.

However, she was adamant, the wedding date was set, and we were informed.

There was nothing more that our father could do.

With one daughter happily married with his blessing in America, one daughter about to commit an 'immoral' contract in marriage, one daughter causing problems at home and needing to be 'carefully watched over' and one daughter fully loyal and pleasing, his troubles were far from over, and every day without fail he would mention his worries in his prayers at family worship.

As the time drew close for the marriage to take place, it was not decided who, if any of us should attend. Our father did not regard it as 'morally correct' but knowing that the law of the land would respect it, both parties being of age and taking part willingly, he knew that he had very little ground for support, in society or in the church. This was truly a case of the "state of Christendom" working against the principles of godliness. All his problems were the fault of the "state of Christendom".

Anxiety increased as the set date draw closer, tensions were quietly rising.

But just two weeks before the set date Jim pulled out, leaving our sister to pick up the pieces, whilst our father was quietly giving thanks for answered prayer, whilst our sister's determination never to go back home was set, and she eventually made a life for herself, having her own family.

I continued to struggle on every level physically, mentally, emotionally and also spiritually. I felt as though my conscience had been seared with a hot iron and the molten mess was my burden of guilt.

The one thing I was completely stripped of was any self-respect. Living on the edge had taken a huge toll of my health and well being, and living under the constant watchful and critical eye of my father and my sister, did nothing to ease my acute feeling of guilt.

Maybe they thought I was treated in a manner better than I actually deserved and that they were being very tolerant, but that's certainly not how I experienced life at this point.

I had been troubled by the darkness I felt, wondering if it was because God maybe had removed his love from me. I had felt his love wrap around me, but now I needed the assurance that the experience had not been some sort of emotional disillusionment at a time of heightened stress, so I was very glad that I knew the Scriptures well enough for the words of St Paul to come to mind as I searched my soul. Writing his letter to the Romans he asks:

"who can separate us from the love of God?" and the answer -

"Nothing can separate us"

"neither death, nor life, or angels, nor principalities, nor powers, nor things present, nor things to come, nor height, nor depth, nor any other creature, shall be able to separate us from the love of God" (Romans 8:38-39).

All my worries and objections were silenced, and all I could do was simply embrace that all-encompassing love in faith without questioning, just like 'a little child' and as Jesus said "Unless you become like a little child, you shall not enter the kingdom of heaven".

The timely reminder of the steadfast love of God, encouraged me immensely, but it also wedged in my soul a worrying doubt concerning the coldness I experienced, in the name of God. The "Precept upon precept: line upon line" (Isaiah 28:10) type of Christianity as we experienced it, seemed very heavy in relation to the "weightier matter of the law, judgement, mercy and faith" (Matthew 23:23) and "Mercy rejoiceth against judgement" (James 2:13), meaning mercy is better than judgment.

Slowly I started to explore my thoughts.

I couldn't match the way I had experienced my father implementing his idea of what God wanted, and what I had understood the spirit of what being like Christ was meant to be like.

Intellectually, of course I understood his teachings, but there was something missing and I searched for an answer.

# Chapter Twenty-Four

After our tutor's death, I was still living with the doors of the house locked and the daily routine didn't change.

Now, without our tutor to help with the supper dishes in the evening, I did them on my own, whilst my sister and father continued their sessions of relaxation, reading and talking upstairs, where I would eventually join them.

There were still some issues which really bothered me, and which simmered away in the background as our daily life carried on with momentous monotony.

There was some irony in the fact that now there were little ones in the immediate family as our oldest sister had had two children and we couldn't afford to knit them anything! I had spent the best part of my life up till now making garments for absolutely anyone who would take them, but now – poverty had taken a hard toll and my nieces got nothing.

Our father had a "dose of his own medicine" when his newly acquired daughter-in-law stopped her husband (our brother) from sending any more money back home, quoting "if any would not work, neither should he eat" (2 Thessalonians 3:10) making it clear that our father had a responsibility to work to provide for himself and his family, as indeed our brother was doing.

I couldn't help but think she was right, and I didn't agree with our father's belief that our circumstances were the fault of 'Christendom'.

Our poverty was now quite entrenched.

I also started to ponder about the extent submission was required of us.

The idea that a woman must submit no matter what she was told to do by her god-given head, that her duty began and ended with submission, and that her 'head' was solely responsible for what he told her to do, I simply found too extreme.

One of the most distressing things I found at this time aged 24, and being kept so closely behind closed doors was, that I spent a lot of time knitting socks for our father, milking goats for our own use, washing our own clothes, cooking so that we could and continue to live, clean the house for our own benefit, and this cycle of activity was making life a very insular self-perpetuating one and that was of no benefit to anyone outside of our existence.

I was very bothered by the fact that our household was in no way contributing to society and I thought that as Christians we should be ministering to others as part of our love to God and sharing his love.

Even though, to earn some small money, my sister and I had decided to start a playschool in the local community centre and had a fairly good attendance, it was for one morning a week and all the money we earned went straight to our father for our own keep and even this seemed to be done only so that we could maintain our existence to do it all over again.

When I mentioned this worry to our father and expressed a wish to do something 'useful' he replied:

"But you knit socks for me, don't you".

He had completely missed my point, willingly or otherwise.

I was extremely concerned about my failing health and had visions of how I would be when I was thirty, forty or fifty years old, being here and doing just what I was doing now and all I could see was an old woman who had lost her mind and whose family kept somewhat secure inside the house.

I had heard and been very intrigued by descriptions of the preverbal 'village idiot' from our tutor, and that was the only picture I could see how my life was going to end.

I could feel my nervous strength weakening and was desperate for it not to break, knowing full well that our father would never really recognise or acknowledge any condition of weakness, and that in fact it would give him further reason to put me down.

Although there were now so many differences in thinking between me and our father, the one which had the biggest impact on me, was this fear that I would not be able to hold onto what strength I had left, how fragile I was and how he would respond if I did have a life-changing break-down.

I was now under 7 stone in weight, with thinning hair, no menstruation, and developing oral abscesses. Sleep was short and inconsistent and a chronic supply of adrenalin was still my constant medication.

I struggled deeply with wanting to do what was right, but also stop a process which I truly felt had already started.

It was a mental battle which oscillated between duty, emotions, instinct, fear and back again to 'duty'.

# Chapter Twenty-Five

A few months after our tutor died and was laid to her rest, my father and sister decided to go away for a couple of weeks, and it was arranged that I would stay with John and his sister. John had by this time, seven years on from his proposal, sold his croft and moved into the nearest town. I had the goats to tend to and they would be put to graze in the paddock belonging to the manse, just a stones throw away.

Although glad to be a bit more free than locked behind closed doors, I wasn't too pleased about being thrown back onto the charity of the church members who I had found so difficult to relate to and who I believed, had made a judgement of my person, life and faith on some false information they chose to believe.

However, the arrangements were made and as my family went off in one direction, I went in another - animals in tow.

I tended to the animals in the morning who were not milking at that time of year, and were really enjoying their fresh pasture of grass and wasteland, grazing happily all day in the autumn sunshine. Things with John and his sister were never as they had once been, though there was a politeness, charity and civility shown to each other.

During this break I met the therapist who our tutor had used in her illness and I learned from him that she had asked that he and his family 'look out for me'. She was worried about me and, knowing her prognosis was short wanted me to be looked after.

He didn't understand why she had singled me out and when he asked her, her reply was very clear.

"The older one has her father, the middle one will be alright, but please look after the youngest".

On hearing this I was surprised that our tutor had been so vocal, and to people she hardly knew, she must have been very worried to have done that. I couldn't answer the obvious question of why this request had been made or what it was that worried her so much.

I gave the therapist as brief an account as I could of my situation at home, and I was invited, even encouraged to leave home immediately and stay with them.

Leaving was something I could only think of as happening sometime in the distant future. Leaving would require a whole lot of - - of whatever I hadn't got right now - Courage, bravery, conviction, a clear conscience, strength, energy, focus and faith.

At least if I did leave, I'd know where to go -
'If I did leave'
There is an 'If' there.
The possibility was somewhere there, out of reach, but there somewhere in the far distant time of whenever.

Trying to get someone like the therapist, to understand why I couldn't just walk out, leave and start making a life for myself was almost impossible.

To others it seemed so simple – just get your stuff and walk away.

Understanding what hold the teaching like ours had on the whole make-up of a person, the mind, emotions and especially on ones' conscience was profound and all-embracing, and sometimes staying in the familiar is easier than walking into the unknown.

Others where living in what to me was the unknown, just as I was living in their umknown.

Leaving my home and family was a frightening prospect for me and I knew as a certainty, that if I was to walk away, I would be leaving, not just my life as I knew it, but also the only people I had shared it with. I knew that I would be walking straight into an estrangement with them and although life was tough, I had to question very deeply if losing my family was a price I was prepared to pay.

I loved them, loved my sisters and my father. I wanted to do right by them. I may not have agreed with everything they did, or some of the attitudes they showed, but that didn't mean I didn't love them, and love has a cord of natural bonding which I held onto strongly, and it didn't seem right to cause a break in that bond.

It was very much in the forefront of my thoughts, that I needed to do the right thing however difficult that might be. I wanted to do what God wanted me to do. I didn't want to give my guilty conscience any more weight to carry and risk being broken by it.

I was somehow expecting God to talk to me directly and tell me what to do in some sort of revelation or in a 'still small voice'.

But there was nothing.

I had been taught that god speaks through his word the Bible, and that any other way 'hearing' god was dubious and could be well be a phantom of one's own wishful thinking and imagination, that there was only one certain voice of God. Of course, according to what I had been taught, the Bible told me to stay under my god-given head, be obedient and submissive and that would be blessed and rewarded.

So why couldn't I accept the will of God as taught to me?

I had hoped that there would be a gentle way to leave, and pinned all those hopes on our father agreeing to the request I put to him, which was that I would be allowed to help a family who had four young children and the mother had been diagnosed with cancer and needed help with the family. I had met this family when I was staying with John and my father and sister were away on holiday.

I didn't think a positive response would be very forthcoming, but when I got the definitive negative answer, it sealed everything I needed to know.

Not for the first time I knew that his way of being a Christian was definitely not the kind I wanted to identify with.

When it suited our father it had been alright for my sisters to go to America and help out with families over there, but for some reason it wasn't alright for me to help this family.

Whether because it was me that was asking, whether it was because the help needed was not in America but in this country, whatever the reason, I made the resolution quietly within myself, that I was going to do it anyway whatever he said.

I talked myself stronger into my resolution, knowing that I would need all the strength I could muster, and knew the price I needed to pay.

The time had come for me to carry out the decision I had made to leave.

Once my decision was made to leave and the struggles with my conscience were answered, the matter of how to execute it seemed so much easier.

But how was this going to be possible?

I had been given the phone number of the therapist our tutor had visited and now, with it tucked into my pocket with a message attached, I handed it to our neighbour as my sister and I bought eggs from her.

The message I wrote was for our neighbour to please phone the number written down and say that I would be ready for pick-up by the war memorial at 1.00am the next night.

My commitment to leave was now made and having involved other people there was no backing out.

I was going, hoping for the best and that it was the right decision.

I knew there would be different opinions about it, I had already met that, but what mattered to me most was that I would get out and retain some sort of integrity.

I knew I would be 'chewed up and had for Sunday lunch' by many, but I couldn't worry about that too much now.

Our tutor had gone and she would have been the one person I would have stayed for, to avoid hurting her, but now was the time for action and if there needed to be regrets, they had to come later.

During the next day at different intervals, I put a few things in a couple of bags and put the bags in a disused room at the back of the house.

Of course I was very worried and nervous that the bags might be seen and my plans uncovered, but I was used to nervous energy, it's what I survived on.

I had calculated the risk and decided it was worth it.

If my plan was discovered, it was discovered and there was nothing left in me to worry about things which may not materialise.

My plans in the evening were helped by my sister and father going out in the car to the phone – a call-box a mile away, and I took the opportunity to go into my father's room and look for a key to the back door.

There on his desk was the back-door key!

I opened the back door, and put the key back on the desk exactly where I had found it.

They returned home while I was still washing up the dishes from supper.

Going through family worship in our father's bedroom/study that evening was very emotional.

Yes, I felt a bit of a hypocrite, knowing that I was planning this to be the last time I would experience something that had been woven in the very fabric of my life since I had been eight years old. That it would be the last time that I would sit on my father's bed, sing Psalms and hear him read. The last time I would be - - - - the last time for life as I knew it.

More certain was the life I was about to leave, than the one I was going forward to.

I had coped with the unknown many, many times in my life so the unknown wasn't as intimidating for me as it might have been, but I was tired, weary and nervous and didn't know how many more changes I could go through.

All my strength was needed for the one step ahead.

After family worship I went to my room knowing, though not certain, that it would be the last time I would sleep in that cold, icy, sparsely furnished room, but my room nonetheless.

Would I ever be make patterns in icy windows again?

Would I ever kneel at this bedside and make my devotions to God?

Not if my plans were going to be successful, and if they weren't then no doubt this room would become my world once again.

I was very determined not to sleep through this one chance I had to make a difference for myself, and refused to allow myself to sleep at all.

Not sure how much time I would need to get up and out of the house, I decided to make a move the minute I knew my father was either in bed or well settled into his room and unlikely to come out.

What posed the biggest risk now was either me making enough noise to wake someone up and of them coming out of their room to find out what was going on, or of one of them needing to use the bathroom, which was downstairs and they would find me all dressed up ready to go somewhere.

Having dressed with as many layers as I could possible fit onto my small frame and still move, I opened my bedroom door and peeked out, ears and eyes peeled for any sign of movement.

All was quiet.

I has hoping that the night wouldn't be one of those very still silent nights, the silence of which would amplify any noise I made.

What would be helpful would be a night of high winds which would make all sorts of howls, noises and creeks in the house and any noise I made would become indistinguishable from natures contribution.

It was neither. The wind was moderate to quiet, which meant that I had to be extremely careful and very quiet indeed.

I put one foot forward.

What do I do with my bedroom door – leave it open with the possibility of it banging shut with a gust of wind, or risk making noise closing it?

There were just some things I hadn't thought of!

If I left it open, any draught might make it slam, but closing the door quietly would take up precious time.

I had loads of time before being picked up, but not to spend it hanging around doing these risqué movements.

I wanted to be up and out as quickly as possible.

I chose to close the door calculating the risk.

I placed another foot forward onto the bare floorboards and was one pace nearer the staircase.

Then onto the first stair and I was on my way!

So near, yet so far.

With the whole bare wooden staircase to descend ahead of me I had a long way to go.

I knew this staircase very well – I had spent many hours cleaning it!

I thought I knew the creak of each one, where it was on the tread and how loud it was. Each step was like a little character, squeaking it's own volume and creaking in its own individual place.

It was most important now that I remembered where each step made a noise, and I needed to avoid the area.

I made another step down. Then another.

I wondered if I could possible take two steps at a time as this was tortuous, but decided that I wouldn't have the necessary control over where and how I landed on the lower step.

The risks had to be weighed up.

Time versus noise.

Expletives were not part of our vocabulary, but had they been, then this journey down the stairs would have been a very colourful one!

I held my breath trying to remember where the noisy part of the next step was but I couldn't remember.

Taking a chance I lowered my right foot as slowly as possible.

Creak.

There it was. I had trodden on the creaky bit, and I stopped in my tracks looking at my sisters bedroom door expecting it to open.

The door didn't move and neither did she.

I continued more cautiously.

This was taking such a long time.

Step by slow step I made my way down.

With every inch forward, my ears and eyes were peeled and my nerves alert.

Slowly but surely I was getting down the stairs and closer to the outside.

I had to stay focused and also think of something to say to the person who might possibly find me.

So long as I was on the staircase and someone came down, I would go on to the bathroom, but once I was in the hallway and trying to open the noisiest door in the whole house, that would need another explanation and one I just couldn't think of.

Finally last the step was trodden and I was on the hall floor safely.

Now to negotiate the hardest part.

Even at the noisiest of times, this door could be heard opening.

It always creaked, cracked and groaned on its hinges and now I had to go through without it making a sound.

I had allowed myself plenty of time.

I took hold of the handle and turned it.

Clonk, the handle went in my hand. Clonk again as I turned a little more.

I was getting even more nervous now.

Would it all come to an end at the last hurdle?

The wind had died down a bit, and the noise of the handle turning was accentuated in the echo created in the eerie silence.

I had to carry on, as the handle would make a noise whatever way it turned, back or forwards, so I may as well keep going forwards.

I squeezed through the doorway but my hand was still on the other side of the door and at a very awkward angle but I dare not change it and make any unnecessary noise.

I would have to let go of the handle, if I wanted to get through, so I did very very slowly to avoid the clank, clank which sounded very loud to me, no doubt magnified by my nerves.

Getting a grip of the other side of the handle, I managed to close the door.

Finally after almost an hour and I was through!

I now had the much simpler part of collecting my bags, opening the back door and walking up to the war memorial and in the darkness of the night I took my two bags and went to meet the person who had agreed to pick me up.

I had made it in plenty of time and now realised the enormity of what was really facing me.

I left a note in my bedroom addressed to my father apologising for the need to leave, but not saying where I was going.

# Chapter Twenty-Six

I had walked away from one life, the only life I had known and had spent so much energy fighting for, thinking it was right, and I entered into a whole new world I knew nothing about.

I hadn't given much thought about what life would be like away from home, or how I would adjust, or even if I would be able to adjust sufficiently to make it.

I just knew that I needed to change my life before it changed me.

The first thing I had to address after leaving home was the care of my goat herd. I knew there was no way my sister would adopt them, so I made arrangements for them to be moved to where I was staying. I advertised them for sale as one herd not to be divided, and was very happy to find a buyer almost immediately and they went to their new home without much disturbance to them.

To the family who took me in immediately after I left home, I must have been an anomaly in every way. There were so many ways in which we were completely different and that made understanding each other quite difficult. Initially I was completely exhausted and rested in my room a lot of the time, but it wasn't long before I was expected to join in everything and take part in what to me was a very noisy and restless family.

This was a christian family, but they were far from what I had been used to in their style of worship, which was a 'church' meeting they held in their home. They sang hymns, but not the ones I had known, they used a modern song book which had many small chorus verses which would often be sung over and over again, in what to me seemed very much to be in the category of 'vain repetition' which I found unintelligent, childlike and quite frankly embarrassing. The raising of the arms and hands in what was thought to be adoring worship, I thought of as exhibitionism and highly distasteful. The freedom with which people would go in and out of the room during worship was something I found totally out of order and disrespectful and unnecessary in the extreme, not to mention highly distracting and annoying.

Then there was the 'speaking in tongues' which I initially found excruciating to have to listen to and appear to appreciate. There was absolutely no way I was going to end up babbling unintelligently in public.

The teaching of St Paul to the Corinthians allows for speaking in tongues in public, but only if there is an interpreter present, and if there is not an interpreter present then the person wanting to speak in tongues should speak to themselves – and yes, I had to agree with St Paul.

Woman speaking and almost leading the service through music I tolerated more, but still it was a big change to adjust to.

I would have been more comfortable if I had been left to adjust to the changes in my own time, as there was a huge amount for me to process, but I felt the pressure to conform, and if I did conform then I would be given the 'gift' of speaking in tongues, and that I would experience visions, revelations and healing and all that was needed on my part was faith in Jesus and openness to the Holy Spirit's work.

My hosts expressed their wish that I would be 'free' free to praise the Lord and prayed over me to release me from the power of darkness.

What they didn't seem to be appreciate was how well versed I was in theology, including theirs and I knew the Biblical arguments for and against practices they engaged in, and that my reticence to fully participate and 'open myself' was from an educated premise, and also a cultural preference, but most importantly I was still sore from being judged in my spiritual life and having attitudes, ideas and practices foisted on me.

Our family had never used raised voices or argued in the home, but this family I was staying with, would often have loud verbal arguments among themselves. All sorts of names and emotions would come out during these arguments, but they were also extremely loyal to each other, and would support each other no-matter what. Initially I found the loudness and aggression very difficult to cope with and something I judged as being not suitable behaviour for people who called themselves christian, but then I thought about what was more important – by being open with each other they were in fact being more honest, than we had ever been with each other, as we had an outward cloak of 'meek and mild' demeanour, which hadn't always reflected the true person, and I realised that we didn't know each other as well as we thought we did.

I had to get used to the way food was treated by this family and by many of the members of their fellowship. To me it was sacrilege to waste food and I was now seeing waste of a very regular basis. Potatoes were peeled thickly in haste, when I would take much longer and peel them so thinly that the skins were transparent! The juice of tinned fruit was tipped down the sink! Food left over from a meal was never kept for another day, but thrown away. For someone who had experienced such a deep hunger as I had, the food wastage was something I simply couldn't get used to and actually didn't want to get used to.

The matter of my clothes was something which the teenagers of my hosts found to be very amusing, which I didn't appreciate at all. Shortly after I arrived on the charity of this fellowship, I was given a full bag of clothes which was really helpful as I had taken almost nothing with me from home, but at the same time they were clothes which were so different from anything I had ever worn, that I felt incredibly embarrassed and uncomfortable wearing them. The skirts and jumpers were bold and brightly coloured, the coat was plastic feeling, puffy and bright and shorter than useful. I couldn't wait to be able to choose my own clothes one day, but for now, everything was gratefully received.

I drew the line at wearing make-up though, feeling that it was one change too many being thrown at me.

I had been taken to the hairdresser to have my long hair cut short which was a huge challenge to get used to, as it hadn't been short since I was about six years old. I was expected to conform to what they wanted and I thought it was a good idea to try different things. But I realised that I had met with intolerance again - an intolerance of anything which was different or outside of their understanding, and I needed to take time to learn who I really was.

There was a loneliness I deeply felt, even though I was constantly surrounded by a very active family who had a constant stream of visitors. I had left those who I had shared my life with, now there was no-one who knew what I had really been through, no matter how they might try and understand. They didn't really know me like my own family did, we hadn't been through anything together, there was no history between us, and that feeling of aloneness was something I was wasn't prepared for at all. Nothing could make up for it and nothing would fill that gap, and there were times when I had had enough of being with a family I didn't know, didn't have much in common with, and I longed for my own family, just to be with my own family again.

After a few months with this family it was time I started to think about how I was going to contribute to my keep, support myself in the future and move on.

As soon as I had arrived, I had applied for unemployment benefit, which was granted to me on the understanding that I would either go into 'further education' or look for employment.

I chose to go into further education and enrolled in the local Technical College to gain some qualifications. I chose to do A level Biology and Scottish Highers in Anatomy and Physiology, with the end goal of studying Medical Herbalism.

My love for learning was satisfied while I studied and I put a lot of effort into the coursework. I was very grateful to our teacher for the energy and time which she put into a rather wayward class of mostly teenagers, and I was determined to do her proud by passing the exams, which I am glad to say I did.

I moved into my first home while studying at the collage, the rent being paid for by adding Housing Benefit to my Unemployment Benefit. It was a small terraced cottage, comprising of a sitting/bedroom, kitchen and bathroom. The cottage was heated by an enjoyable coal fire in the sitting room, which I used to love sitting beside and absorbing all the heat from it that I could.

I had all I needed and was getting stronger by the day. I budgeted well, having a coin meter for electricity, and buying coal from the merchant behind the cottage. I would often cycle to the college to save money, which was a ride of about 5 miles each way or if the weather was too wet I would take a bus.

I naturally got in touch with our mother after I left home. I went to visit her in London and she visited me as well. We exchanged our life's experiences and learned a lot about each other. She had no idea how things had developed with our father since her visit to us in our home with our tutor so many years ago, and I had no idea that although my father in their divorce proceedings had been awarded legal custody of all his children, she had actually been awarded equal visitation rights.

Finding a huge amount of courage one day I decided to visit my father and sister and cycled over to the house. The air between us was frosty and my sister, not surprisingly, viewed me with suspicion, while my father made it very clear to me that I had broken the moral order and it would only be a matter of time before I experienced God's punishment. He also said that although I shouldn't have left, by leaving I had made things easier for him as he had 'one less mouth to feed'.

As far as I was concerned, the God I believed in was a God of mercy, so I could willingly accept whatever he wanted to give me.

I had wanted to get some of my possessions from the house, but I was not allowed to touch anything. I was told that what I had left, I had willingly left and it now reverted to being our fathers possession.

There was a knock on the front door of my cottage one day and I was very surprised to see my sister on the doorstep with a pile of clothes in her hand. She sheepishly asked if she could iron the pile of clothes she was carrying using my iron, and offered to put a coin in the meter.

Electricity in their own house had once again been cut off. I couldn't refuse, but didn't want to be in the house while she did her ironing, so I went out for a walk and returned while she was waiting for our father to pick her up. Were we slowly finding our way to some sort of reconciliation?

My father and sister would sometimes attend the evening service of the church which was only a street away from my cottage, and which we had been going to for years.

After the service they would come and visit me, sitting by my warm fire for a couple of hours. There was no heavy conversation at all, no theology, we were just spending time together over some supper, which was my father's favourite on a Sunday evening – a bowl of Scottish porridge made by me who had been doing it for years and had perfected it his liking.

In the college I attended, one of the technicians was an elder of the church we had attended, and which my father and sister were still going to sometimes, but which I had stopped going to when I left home. One day, as we passed each other in the college corridor, he made a point of stopping and talking to me, which was something I had wanted to avoid. He told me that the church (the elders) understood my position and would I consider going back to the church? This was the church and the elders who had asked that I abstain from taking communion a couple of years previously. They may have 'understood' my position, but in no way was I ready to think about returning to worship with them and relive all the memories of the past.

To continue my training in the School of Herbal Medicine, I needed to attend a viable clinic and do 500 clinical training hours, so I started to look at moving South to England where there were many more clinics able to accommodate and teach students.

My mother's brother had invited to me to stay in the top floor of his house which I was very grateful to accept, and so it was with anticipation that I packed my little cottage into a car and drove down South.

Before I left my cottage to move south, I had a visit from John, who I hadn't seen much of since my removal to England aged 17. I was now 25 years old and John had retired and was suffering from very poor eyesight. He had heard that I was moving away and had come to say goodbye, which he did in the words

"If I was forty years younger, I won't let you go".

In that fleeting moment of tenderness, I sensed his compassion, his understanding and his true reaction to all that had happened. Nothing had changed his feelings. He had remained as true to himself - and to what we had, as I knew he would.

The one thing I really wanted my father to grasp and understand, was that although I had walked out from under his authority I had in no way given up the faith. I still had a loyalty to and a faith in God and that I hadn't 'proselytised myself with the world' to use his own phrase.

God had me in his grasp and wasn't about to let go and although my love had faltered, the faith I had come to share as a young child remained.

# The afterwards

I have been asked, and indeed I have asked myself many times, how does one adjust to a 'normal life' after such a sheltered and yet dramatic childhood?

It certainly doesn't happen by going into a clinic in one state of mind and leaving after many sessions with a different mind-set. No, it takes a lot of time, reflection, and continuous hard work, but most of all it takes time.

In many ways my life would have been much easier if I had been able to dismiss religion in all is forms after I left the family home, as that would have been a cleaner break, but I couldn't. I have a deep faith and belief in God which started from a tender age, and I can't deny that faith, just because I experienced a few difficulties in connection with it. My faith is very personal to me and something which I needed to find a way of expressing without imposing on others.

Consequently, it was not easy for me to know what aspects I needed to take from my childhood, what ideas, principles, ideals or habits to carry forward, and what I needed to leave behind, and that process took many years to work out.

In time, I was able to connect with my father and sister as it was most important to me they understood, that although I had left them, in doing so I had not forsaken the faith that we shared.

The attachment I felt to my natural family was very strong indeed, and this attachment and love, together with the need I had of their approval remained very high. However that attachment also made it very difficult for me to be clear about what I wanted and needed in life. In my mind I had one idea, but my heart was often telling me something else and it was a long time before I was working as one unit.

The legacy of my childhood has been an incredibly deep and lasting absence of self-worth. Having almost no self-respect, I often looked for recognition and validation from other people, and this would sometimes be painfully disappointing and enervating.

I had learned very early in life to take everything very seriously indeed, and it has taken many years to learn not to put too much weight on what other people say. I tended to believe that what anyone said to me was de facto the truth and I would react accordingly, when in fact what they said was often only their opinion, and opinions are only things which are formed, often by inexperience and the transient nature of being human. This tendency led me to being troubled about things which I heard and took seriously. It had become second nature to me to hear something and react like it was the absolute truth almost before I realised how I had reacted. I also had become a sponge for absorbing guilt and these two things put together, made life very difficult. I was hyper-sensitive to criticism and became depressed with guilt – justified or not.

The natural cheekiness which my mother describes me possessing as a young toddler, was sadly suppressed in me for many years, and I have gone through times when showing any form of happiness seemed inappropriate and it was a long time before I realised that sadness and joy can be held in parallel to each other – at the same time, that they are not mutually exclusive.

I have been blessed with a strong spirit of resilience and fortitude, which has been much needed throughout my life, and has been called on again and again in many different circumstances, and has helped me through the past six decades.

www.ingramcontent.com/pod-product-compliance
Lightning Source LLC
Chambersburg PA
CBHW071446070526
44578CB00001B/233